Italian Casserole Cooking

Italian
Casserole Cooking

ANGELA CATANZARO

LIVERIGHT

NEW YORK

Contents

Introduction

The rich and varied culinary heritage of Italy has produced a vast collection of one-dish specialty meals. The recipes in this book are among the most representative of the various classic regional dishes of Italy.

Casseroles are time-savers for the busy housewife, yet they can be elegant and subtle, combining many interesting flavors, textures, colors and aromas. Most of the casseroles in this book can be prepared within an hour; many can be prepared in advance and refrigerated or frozen. Most casseroles require only a salad, bread, dessert and a beverage to round out the menu and produce an appealing table.

Most of the casserole recipes included are ideal for outdoor dining and large gatherings. They provide the hostess, as well as her guests, with a carefree evening of enjoyment. You can expect these casseroles to become family "favorites" as well as entertainment specialties.

These recipes will offer some challenge to even the most epicurean of palates. They bear out the firm Italian belief that food is at its best when eaten "all'Italiana"—Italian style.

I exhort you to eat heartily of these fine dishes—as the Italians do.

Angela Catanzaro

Beef

BEEFSTEAK PIZZAIOLA

Bistecca alla Pizzaiola

4 tablespoons olive oil
2 lbs. top round steak,
   about ½ inch thick, cut
   into 4 pieces
1 clove garlic, chopped, or
   1 medium onion, thinly
   sliced

3½ cups tomatoes (#2½
   can)
1 teaspoon salt
¼ teaspoon pepper or to
   taste
1 teaspoon oregano
4 tablespoons grated
   Parmesan cheese
   (optional)

Heat oil in electric frying pan or heavy skillet. Brown meat on both sides over low fire (about 15 minutes). In last minute of browning add garlic or onion, tomatoes, salt, pepper and oregano. Cover and cook for 1 hour or until meat is tender, stirring occasionally. If sauce gets too dry, add ½ cup water. Sauce can be served with 1 8-oz. package noodles or elbow macaroni cooked according to directions on label of package. Sprinkle with grated Parmesan cheese if desired. Preparing this dish well in advance will enhance the flavor. May be frozen. Serves 4.

NOTE: Veal chops or pork chops may also be prepared according to above recipe.

Cook's Notes:

BEEFSTEAK AND POTATOES

Bistecca con Patate

1 small onion, finely
  chopped
½ cup Romano or
  Parmesan cheese, grated
Salt and pepper to taste
¼ cup parsley, chopped
4 tablespoons leaf lard

2 lbs. round steak, about ½
  inch thick
4 medium potatoes, sliced
  ½ inch thick
½ cup water

Combine onion, cheese, salt, pepper and parsley. **Grease** 2 qt. casserole with 1 tablespoon lard. **Place** meat in casserole and **sprinkle** with half the onion mixture; **add** layer of potatoes and sprinkle with remainder of onion mixture. **Dot** with 3 tablespoons lard. **Bake** uncovered at 375° for 20 minutes. **Add** water and cook 45 or 50 minutes longer or until meat and potatoes are tender. Serves 4–6.

Cook's Notes:

BEEF HOME STYLE

Manzo Famigliare

2–3 lbs. beef chuck, sliced
   ¼ inch thick
¼ cup butter or olive oil
2 large onions, thinly sliced
6 medium potatoes, peeled
   and sliced

2 stalks celery, chopped
1 green pepper, chopped
   (optional)
1 teaspoon salt
⅛ teaspoon pepper
1 cup water or broth

Heat butter or oil in large skillet over medium heat. **Brown** meat 5 minutes on each side. **Spread** onions, potatoes, celery and green pepper over meat. **Season** with salt and pepper. **Add** water or broth. Lower heat and cover tightly. **Simmer** 1¼ hours or until meat and vegetables are tender. Check occasionally. Serves 6.

Cook's Notes:

BEEF PARMESAN

Bistecca Parmigiana

10 small beef cutlets,
pounded very thin
2 eggs, beaten
½ teaspoon salt
⅛ teaspoon pepper
1 cup bread crumbs
1 cup Parmesan cheese,
grated

¼ cup oil
1 cup tomato sauce
6 thin slices mozzarella
cheese
2½ tablespoons Parmesan
cheese, grated

Dip cutlets into beaten egg, then into seasoned bread crumbs mixed with Parmesan cheese. **Sauté** cutlets slowly in oil, browning both sides lightly. **Cover** with tomato sauce and slices of mozzarella cheese. **Sprinkle** with remaining Parmesan cheese and **bake** 15 to 20 minutes at 350°, until cheese is melted and meat is tender. Can be frozen. Serves 5–6.

Cook's Notes:

OVEN BEEF STEW

Umido di Carne

1½ lbs. beef chuck, cut
  into 1-inch cubes
2 tablespoons flour
1½ teaspoons salt
⅛ teaspoon pepper
2 tablespoons lard
1½ cups water
1 tablespoon vinegar

½ cup dry red wine,
  (optional)
1 6-oz. can tomato paste
4 cloves
10 small onions, peeled
6 carrots, peeled and cut
  lengthwise into quarters
1 10-oz. package frozen
  peas, thawed

Mix flour, salt and pepper. **Dredge** beef in flour mixture. Melt lard in skillet. **Brown** beef for 10 minutes over medium heat, turning occasionally. **Turn into** casserole. In same skillet, **add** water and scrape up browned drippings. **Stir in** vinegar, wine, tomato paste; add cloves. **Bring to boil. Surround** meat with onions, carrots and peas. **Pour** tomato mixture over all. **Bake** at 350° for 1½ hours or until meat is tender. Can be prepared in advance and refrigerated. If refrigerated, allow 15 minutes more baking time. Serves 4.

Cook's Notes:

BEEF UMBRIAN STYLE

Manzo alla Umbria

4 slices (about ¼ lb.) salt pork, cut into 1-inch pieces
2 lbs. boneless chuck, bottom round or beef stew, cut into 1½-inch cubes
1 teaspoon salt or to taste
⅛ teaspoon pepper
1 large onion, sliced
1 clove garlic, chopped
1 cup beef stock or bouillon
1 cup canned tomatoes
3 whole cloves
½ bay leaf
½ cup red wine
3 stalks celery
3 carrots
3 potatoes, peeled and quartered (optional)

Place salt pork in Dutch oven or heavy skillet. **Cook** until crisp. **Remove** salt pork and **stir in** meat. Sprinkle with salt and pepper. **Cook** over medium heat until meat loses red color (about 10 minutes), stirring frequently for 1 minute. In last minute of cooking **add** onion and garlic, beef stock or bouillon, tomatoes, cloves, bay leaf and wine. Stir. Cover tightly and reduce heat. **Simmer** 1½ hours.

Meanwhile **wash and cut** celery stalks into 2-inch pieces. **Scrape** carrots and slice into 2-inch pieces. **Add** these to meat and **cook** 30 minutes longer or until meat and vegetables are tender; if desired **add** 3 peeled and quartered potatoes. **Discard** bay leaf. Serve hot. Preparing this dish a day ahead of time and reheating it will improve the flavor. May be frozen, omitting potatoes. Serves 4–6.

VARIATIONS: *With Lamb*

Substitute 2 lbs. boned lamb shoulder for beef, and 1 tablespoon leaf lard or butter for salt pork. Before serving, **spoon off** any excess fat that has risen to the surface.

With Veal

Substitute 2 lbs. boned lamb shoulder for beef, and 1 tablewine.

Cook's Notes:

MEAT PEASANT STYLE

Carne alla Paesana

2 lbs. bottom round or
  chuck, cut into 2-inch
  pieces
1 tablespoon oil or leaf lard
4 cups hot water
2 medium turnips
2 medium parsnips
1 sweet red pepper, pith
  and seeds removed

4 stalks celery
2 medium onions
3 medium potatoes
2 beef bouillon cubes
⅛ teaspoon basil or
  marjoram
1 tablespoon salt or to taste
¼ teaspoon pepper

Heat oil or lard in casserole or heavy saucepan. **Brown** meat over medium heat until well-browned on all sides (about 10 to 12 minutes). **Stir** occasionally. **Add** water and cover. Reduce heat and **simmer** for 1½ hours or until fork tender, adding more water if necessary. Meanwhile **peel** vegetables and **cut** into cubes. **Add** vegetables, bouillon cubes, herbs and seasonings. **Stir** to blend. Recover and **cook** 30 minutes longer or until meat and vegetables are tender. May be frozen omitting potatoes; preparing this dish in advance will enhance flavor. Serves 4–6.

NOTE: Veal or lamb may be prepared in the same way.

Cook's Notes:

MEAT WITH SAUCE

Carne con Salsa

1 chuck or round steak
(3–4 lbs) about 1 inch
thick
3 tablespoons oil
2 cloves garlic
4 potatoes, peeled and
sliced about ¼ inch
thick
½ cup beef bouillon or
water

1 cup tomato sauce or 1
8-oz. can of tomato sauce
⅛ teaspoon oregano
(optional)
Salt and pepper to taste
3 tablespoons Parmesan
cheese, grated (optional)

Heat oil in large skillet over medium fire. **Sauté garlic** 1 minute. Push aside garlic or discard if desired. **Brown** meat in same oil until brown on both sides (about 10 to 15 minutes). **Transfer** meat to oblong casserole or 13×9×2 inch pan. Top meat with sliced potatoes. **Add** remaining ingredients. **Bake** at 350° for 1¼ hours or until meat and potatoes are tender. Can be frozen without the potatoes. Serves 4–6.

VARIATION: *With Mushrooms and Onions*

2 tablespoons oil or butter
1 lb. fresh mushrooms, sliced

3 medium onions, thinly
sliced

While meat is browning, **sauté** mushrooms and onions for 5 minutes in oil or butter in separate pan over low heat, turning occasionally. **Omit** potatoes. May be frozen.

Cook's Notes:

OXTAIL RAGOUT

Ragu di Coda

2 slices bacon, cut into
small pieces
1 tablespoon leaf lard
3 lbs. oxtails, cut into
2-inch pieces
2 medium onions, chopped
2 stalks celery, cut into
2-inch pieces

½ clove garlic, minced
(optional)
1 medium carrot, chopped
1 tablespoon parsley,
chopped
1 cup canned tomatoes
Salt and pepper to taste
⅛ teaspoon nutmeg
(optional)
1 cup dry red wine
3 cups beef bouillon or
water

Place bacon, lard, oxtails, onions, celery, garlic, carrot and parsley in Dutch oven or heavy saucepan. **Brown** over medium heat, turning occasionally, for about 10 minutes. **Add** remaining ingredients. Cover and reduce heat. **Cook** slowly 3 hours or until meat falls off bones. **Skim off** excess fat before serving. Preparing well in advance enhances flavor. Can be frozen. Serves 4–6.

NOTE: Can also be baked at 300° for 3 hours. Use large casserole or bake in Dutch oven.

Serving suggestion: Serve over rice or noodles.

Cook's Notes:

BEEF STEW

Manzo Spezzato

2 lbs. boned chuck or
   bottom round, cut into
   2-inch cubes
3 tablespoons olive oil
2 medium onions, sliced
1 clove garlic
1 tablespoon parsley,
   chopped
1 cup diced celery

2 cups hot water or
   bouillon
1 teaspoon lemon
1 bay leaf
3–4 medium potatoes,
   peeled and quartered
4 carrots, peeled and cut
   into 2-inch pieces
Salt and pepper to taste
1 cup burgundy

Brown meat in oil in large heavy skillet or Dutch oven, over
low heat (about 20 minutes), turning often for even browning.
Add onion, garlic, parsley and celery; sauté 5 minutes. Add water
or bouillon, lemon and bay leaf. Cover and **cook** slowly 45 minutes, stirring occasionally. **Remove** garlic and bay leaf. **Add**
chopped vegetables to meat. **Season** with salt and pepper. **Add**
wine. Cover and **simmer** 30 to 45 minutes or until meat and
vegetables are tender. Can be frozen (omitting potatoes) for
later use. Serves 6.

NOTE: Lamb or veal may be used instead of beef.

Cook's Notes:

SAVORY POT ROAST

Manzo alla Lombarda

4 lbs. beef chuck, rump or
  round
4 tablespoons leaf lard,
  bacon fat or oil
1 medium onion, coarsely
  chopped

¼ cup water
1 6-oz. can sliced
  mushrooms, with liquid
1 teaspoon salt
⅛ teaspoon pepper
⅛ teaspoon nutmeg
  (optional)

Heat lard, bacon fat or oil in Dutch oven or deep, heavy pot with tight-fitting lid. **Sear** meat over high heat, turning to brown on all sides (about 5 to 7 minutes). **Add** remaining ingredients and cover tightly. **Cook** slowly on top of stove or bake at 300° for 3 to 4 hours or until meat is almost tender, turning several times during cooking. Remove meat to hot platter. Can be frozen. Serves 6.

VARIATION: *With Vegetables*

4 medium potatoes, peeled
  and quartered
4 medium carrots, scraped
  and cut into 2-inch pieces

4 stalks celery, cut into
  2-inch pieces
4 small onions, peeled

Arrange vegetables around meat 45 minutes before meat is done. If freezing this variation, omit potatoes. (Add potatoes just before placing pot roast in oven to reheat.)

Cook's Notes:

BEEF TRENTINO STYLE

Manzo alla Trentina

3 lbs. chuck or bottom
round, cut into 2-inch
cubes
3 tablespoons butter or
bacon drippings
1½ teaspoons salt

⅛ teaspoon pepper
2 medium onions, sliced
2 cups bouillon or water
2 tablespoons tomato paste
or 2 fresh tomatoes,
peeled and finely chopped

Heat butter or bacon drippings in Dutch oven or heavy skillet. Brown meat cubes on all sides (about 15 minutes). Sprinkle with salt and pepper. Add onions and cook 3 minutes longer, stirring frequently. Add bouillon or water and tomato paste or fresh tomatoes. Cover tightly. Simmer slowly 1 hour or until meat is tender. Can be frozen for later use. Serves 6.

Serving suggestion: Serve with 8-oz. package hot cooked noodles.

Cook's Notes:

ITALIAN STYLE SHORT RIBS

Cotolette all'Italiana

2 lbs. short ribs, cut into
  2-inch pieces
1 tablespoon butter
⅛ lb. salt pork, chopped, or
  3 slices bacon
1½ teaspoons salt
⅛ teaspoon pepper

1 cup bouillon or soup
  broth
2 tablespoons lemon juice
¼ cup burgundy or any
  red wine
⅛ teaspoon marjoram or
  oregano (optional)

Place short ribs, butter and salt pork or bacon in heavy skillet or saucepan. **Brown** about 10 minutes over medium heat, stirring constantly. **Transfer** ribs and fat to 2-qt. casserole. **Sprinkle** with salt and pepper. **Add** remaining ingredients and cover. (If casserole has no lid, cover with aluminum foil.) **Bake** at 350° for 1½ to 2 hours. (Cooking time depends on thickness of meat when it begins to separate from bones.) **Spoon off** excess fat and serve from casserole. Serves 4.

NOTE: May also be prepared on top of stove in heavy skillet or Dutch oven.

Serving suggestion: Serve with Broccoli Parmesan and hot cooked rice prepared with some of remaining pan juices.

VARIATION: *With Vegetables*

4 small onions, peeled
4 medium potatoes, peeled
   and quartered

3 medium carrots, peeled
   and sliced
1 10-oz. box frozen peas or
   green beans (optional)

Add vegetables to meat 30 minutes before meat is done. Cook until meat and vegetables are tender. (It may be necessary to use larger casserole.)

Serving suggestion: Serve with tossed salad and crusty Italian bread.

Cook's Notes:

BAKED ROUND STEAK

Bistecca al Forno

2 lbs. round steak, 1 inch
  thick, cut into serving
  pieces
¼ cup flour
2 tablespoons Parmesan
  cheese, grated
¼ teaspoon thyme
1 teaspoon salt
⅛ teaspoon pepper
¼ cup olive oil

1 clove garlic, minced
1 6-oz. can tomato paste
1½ cups water
¼ teaspoon sugar
¼ teaspoon salt
⅛ teaspoon pepper
1 bay leaf
2 green peppers, cut into
  rings
2 medium onions, sliced

Combine in bowl flour, cheese, thyme, 1 teaspoon salt and pepper. **Dredge** steak with flour. **Heat** oil in large skillet. **Brown** steak 5 minutes on each side. **Remove** to casserole. In same skillet, **stir in** garlic, tomato paste and water. **Add** sugar, salt, pepper and bay leaf. **Bring to boil. Pour** over meat. **Arrange** pepper rings and onions on top of meat. **Bake** at 450° for 1½ to 2 hours or until meat is tender. Can be prepared in advance and refrigerated or frozen. (If refrigerated, allow 15 minutes more for baking.) Serves 4–6.

Serving suggestion: Serve with ½ lb. hot cooked medium noodles. Spoon sauce over noodles.

Cook's Notes:

BRAISED BEEF

Manzo Brasato

3–4 lbs. rump or chuck
  roast
2 tablespoons flour
Salt and pepper to taste
¼ cup oil, butter or bacon
  fat
1 cup beef broth or water

1 small onion, minced
1 small carrot, minced
1 stalk celery, minced
2 whole cloves
1 cup red wine

Combine flour, salt and pepper. Sprinkle on waxed paper or platter. **Roll** meat in seasoned flour mixture. **Heat** oil, butter or bacon fat in a Dutch oven or heavy saucepan with tight cover. **Brown** meat well on all sides over medium heat about 15 to 20 minutes. Add remaining ingredients. **Simmer** over low heat 1½ to 2½ hours or until meat is tender. Remove meat to serving platter. Can be prepared one day ahead of time or may be frozen. Serves 6.

VARIATION: **Add** 1 cup tomatoes with remaining ingredients.

Serving suggestion: Serve with boiled rice or potatoes.

Cook's Notes:

STUFFED MEAT LOAF

Polpettone Ripieno

2 lbs. meat loaf mixture
  (ground beef, pork and
  veal)
1 cup bread crumbs
2 eggs
1 teaspoon salt
1/4 teaspoon freshly ground
  pepper
1/2 teaspoon basil
Grated rind of 1 lemon
1 small onion, grated

1 clove garlic, minced
2 tablespoons parsley,
  minced
1/2 cup Fontina or
  Parmesan cheese, grated
2 hard-boiled eggs, sliced
1 6-oz. package Provolone,
  sliced
1/4 lb. salami, diced
2 tablespoons butter
1 cup bouillon

Place ground meat in bowl with bread crumbs, eggs, salt, pepper, basil, lemon rind, onion, garlic, parsley and grated cheese. **Mix** thoroughly with hands. On waxed paper, **pat** meat mixture into 10×12 inch rectangle. **Place** sliced eggs and Provolone lengthwise on top of mixture. **Sprinkle on** salami. **Roll** meat like jelly roll, using waxed paper as a guide. **Grease** oval casserole or baking pan with butter, and place meat loaf, seam side down in casserole. **Pour** bouillon over meat loaf. **Bake** at 350° about 1¼ hours or until done but not dry. Remove from oven and let stand 10 minutes before serving. Serve hot or cold. Excellent for a buffet. Can be prepared in advance and stored in refrigerator or frozen. Serves 8.

VARIATION: *With Vegetables*

8 small white onions,   8 small carrots, peeled
  peeled   Salt and pepper to taste
8 small potatoes, peeled

Arrange onions, potatoes and carrots around meat loaf.
Sprinkle vegetables with salt and pepper. Follow baking instructions above.

Serving suggestion: Serve with fresh fruit and Gorgonzola cheese.

Cook's Notes:

MEAT LOAF WITH POTATOES

Polpettone con Patate

1½ lbs. ground beef
1 cup bread crumbs
1 tablespoon parsley,
  minced
1½ teaspoons salt
⅛ teaspoon pepper
2 eggs
1 medium onion, finely
  chopped
½ cup water

½ cup Romano cheese,
  grated
2 medium potatoes, peeled,
  cooked, drained and
  mashed
1 cup (¼ lb.) Provolone
  cheese, shredded
4 tablespoons olive oil

Place ground meat in bowl with all ingredients except mashed potatoes, Provolone cheese and oil. **Mix** thoroughly with hands. **Grease** 8×10 inch oblong casserole with 2 tablespoons oil. **Pat** half the meat mixture over bottom of casserole. **Spread** mashed potatoes over this. **Sprinkle** with shredded Provolone. **Cover** with remaining meat mixture and press down edges. **Drizzle** with remaining oil. **Bake** at 350° for 1 hour or until golden brown. Let stand 10 minutes before serving. Can be prepared one day ahead and refrigerated. Serves 4.

VARIATION: *With Ricotta*
  Substitute 1 lb. ricotta or creamy cottage cheese and **omit** mashed potatoes. Proceed in same manner.

Cook's Notes:

Chicken

CHICKEN ABRUZZI

Pollo all'Abruzzi

1 2½–3 lb. fryer, cut into pieces
¼ cup olive oil
1 large onion, chopped
1 cup celery, chopped
1 cup fresh tomatoes, peeled and diced, or 1 cup canned tomatoes

1 cup water
1 tablespoon capers, washed and drained
10 green olives, cut in half
1 tablespoon vinegar
½ teaspoon sugar
Salt and pepper to taste

Wash chicken and dry with paper towels. **Heat** oil in large skillet. **Sauté** chicken on all sides (about 10 minutes). **Add** remaining ingredients. Cover tightly and **simmer** 30 to 45 minutes or until chicken is tender, turning several times. (If desired, transfer chicken and remaining ingredients to 3-qt. casserole. Cover and bake at 350° for 1 to 1½ hours or until chicken is tender.) Preparing chicken well in advance will enhance its flavor. May be frozen indefinitely. Serves 4.

Serving suggestion: Serve with crusty Italian bread.

Cook's Notes:

CHICKEN BREASTS WITH CHEESE

Petti di Pollo con Formaggio

6 chicken breasts, boned and
   cut in half
½ cup flour
½ teaspoon salt
⅛ teaspoon pepper
2 tablespoons Parmesan
   cheese, grated
1 cup butter or margarine

2–3 eggs, beaten
½ lb. fresh mushrooms,
   thinly sliced
1 cup (about ½ lb.)
   cooked ham, diced
1 cup (4 oz.) Provolone or
   Fontina cheese, shredded

Wash chicken breasts and dry with paper towels. **Place** flour, salt, pepper and grated cheese in paper bag or plastic bag. **Shake** chicken breasts until coated with flour mixture. **Melt** butter in large skillet over medium heat. **Dip** floured breasts in beaten egg mixture. **Brown** 10 minutes on each side or until golden brown. **Remove** to casserole or baking pan. In same skillet, **sauté** mushrooms for 5 minutes. **Spoon** mushrooms over chicken. **Sprinkle** with ham and cheese. **Bake** at 350° for 35 to 45 minutes or until tender. May be prepared in advance and refrigerated. (If refrigerated, allow 15 minutes more baking time.) Serves 6.

Serving suggestion: Serve with Risotto.

Cook's Notes:

CHICKEN FERRARA STYLE

Pollo alla Ferrara

3–3½ lb. broiling or
frying chicken, cut into
serving pieces
¼ lb. (½ cup) butter or
margarine
3 medium carrots, scraped
and cut into halves
crosswise

3 medium potatoes, peeled
and cut into halves
½ lb. mushrooms, whole
with stems (optional)
1½ teaspoons salt
⅛ teaspoon pepper
2 tablespoons sherry or
water (if necessary)

Melt butter in saucepan. **Arrange** chicken, skin side down, in
oval casserole or 13×9×2 inch pan. **Arrange** vegetables around
chicken. **Sprinkle** chicken and vegetables with salt and pepper.
Pour melted butter or margarine over chicken and vegetables.
Bake uncovered at 350° for 45 to 60 minutes or until chicken
and vegetables are tender. Do not turn chicken or vegetables.
Sprinkle with sherry or water if needed. Serves 4.

Cook's Notes:

CHICKEN FARFALLE

Pollo con Farfalle

1 2½–3 lb. chicken, cut into serving pieces
¼ cup olive oil
1 teaspoon salt
1 clove garlic
½ cup green pepper, chopped
6 green onions, chopped or ½ cup onion, chopped
1 1-lb. 13-oz. can tomatoes (3½ cups)
1 bay leaf
½ teaspoon thyme
1 tablespoon parsley, chopped
2 tablespoons butter
1 tablespoon flour
½ cup dry white wine
1/16 teaspoon cayenne pepper
8 oz. Farfalle (large bow-tie noodles)
¼ cup grated Parmesan cheese (optional)

Wash chicken and dry with paper towels. **Heat** oil in large heavy skillet, electric frying pan or Dutch oven. **Add** pieces of chicken and sprinkle with salt. Over medium heat, **brown** chicken on all sides (about 10 to 12 minutes). **Remove** chicken and keep hot. In same pan **sauté** garlic, green pepper and onions for 3 minutes. **Add** tomatoes, bay leaf, thyme and parsley, breaking tomatoes with fork. **Return** chicken to skillet. In separate pan, **melt** butter and **stir in** flour. Do not brown. **Add** wine, stirring constantly until mixture is smooth. **Pour** wine and butter mixture over chicken; sprinkle with cayenne. **Turn** chicken and cover tightly. **Cook** slowly on top of stove or in electric skillet 30 to 45 minutes or until chicken is tender.

Cook noodles according to instructions on package until chewey (*al dente*). Drain. On platter, arrange chicken around noodles. Remove bay leaf from sauce; pour sauce over farfalle. (If desired sprinkle with Parmesan cheese.) May be prepared ahead of time, but do not cook noodles until ready to serve. May be frozen indefinitely. Serves 4.

VARIATION: **Substitute** boiled potatoes or elbow macaroni for bow-tie noodles.

Cook's Notes:

CHICKEN MANTUA

Pollo alla Mantova

1 2½–3 lb. chicken, cut
  into pieces
¼ cup olive oil or butter
1 large carrot, scraped and
  diced
1 medium onion, chopped
¼ cup celery, chopped
¼ cup celery leaves, finely
  chopped
1½ teaspoons salt

⅛ teaspoon pepper
1 cup tomato juice
10 black olives, pitted and
  diced
10 green olives, pitted and
  diced
¼ cup sauterne wine
  (optional)
3 cups hot cooked rice (1
  cup uncooked)

Rinse chicken pieces and dry with paper towels. **Heat** oil or melt butter in electric skillet or large flameproof casserole. Arrange chicken pieces skin side up; **brown** over medium heat, turning on all sides (about 10 minutes). **Add** carrot, onion, celery, and celery leaves. **Sprinkle** with salt and pepper. **Cook** 10 minutes. **Add** tomato juice, olives and wine. **Cover and cook** 45 minutes or until fork tender. May be frozen. Serves 4–6.

Serving suggestion: Serve with hot rice.

Cook's Notes:

CHICKEN WITH MOSTACCIOLI

Pollo con Mostaccioli

1 frying chicken (3–3½ lbs.), cut into 8 pieces
3 tablespoons olive oil
2 cloves garlic
1 #2½ can tomatoes or 3½ cups fresh tomatoes, peeled
2 6-oz. cans tomato paste

6 tomato paste cans water
¼ teaspoon basil
Salt and pepper to taste
1 lb. Mostaccioli
½ cup Parmesan or Fontina cheese, grated

Heat oil in large skillet. **Brown** chicken on all sides over medium heat (about 10 minutes). **Transfer** chicken to large, deep, heavy kettle. In same oil **sauté** garlic until brown (about 3 minutes). **Purée** canned or fresh tomatoes in blender or food strainer. **Mix** tomatoes, tomato paste and water with garlic in skillet. **Add** basil, salt and pepper. **Blend** well and pour mixture over chicken. **Simmer** uncovered over low heat for 2½ hours or until thick, stirring frequently to prevent burning.

Cook Mostaccioli in salted boiling water according to directions on label of package. Drain and put into large serving dish. **Pour** half the cheese over Mostaccioli. **Mix** thoroughly with two forks. Serve Mostaccioli in individual dishes; serve chicken separately with some of sauce. Pass rest of sauce and rest of cheese in separate servers. Preparing well in advance enhances flavor. May be frozen. Serves 4–6.

Cook's Notes:

MAMA MIA CHICKEN

Pollo

2 frying chickens (2½–3
  lbs.), quartered
¾ cup soft lard or
  margarine
1 teaspoon salt
⅛ teaspoon pepper
6 medium carrots, peeled
3 medium onions

¼ lb. salami
2 tablespoons oil
1 can (16 oz.) peas,
  undrained
Chicken necks, giblets,
  hearts, livers, washed
½ teaspoon salt
1 cup dry red wine

Wash chicken and dry well with paper towels. **Rub** chicken
pieces inside and out with lard. Sprinkle with salt and pepper.
Arrange chicken, skin side up, in single uncrowded layer in
baking pan or roaster. **Bake** in preheated oven at 350° for 35
to 40 minutes or until chicken is brown, but not done.

Meanwhile, dice carrots, onions and salami in food chopper,
using coarse blade. **Heat** oil in saucepan. **Add** chopped vegetables
and **sauté** 5 minutes, stirring frequently. **Add** peas with liquid,
necks, giblets, hearts and livers. Season with salt. **Cook** over
medium heat 15 minutes. Remove from heat and **stir in** wine.
Add vegetable mixture to browned chicken. Bake 25 minutes
longer or until fork tender. Taste and add more salt and pepper
if necessary. Preparing this dish in advance will enhance flavor.
Can be frozen for later use. Serves 6.

Serving suggestion: Serve with roast potatoes (see p. 151).

Cook's Notes:

CHICKEN WITH MUSHROOMS

Pollo con Funghi

1 2½–3 lb. chicken, cut
into serving pieces
1 medium onion, sliced
6 tablespoons butter or 3
tablespoons butter and 3
tablespoons oil

½ lb. fresh mushrooms
⅛ teaspoon nutmeg
Salt and pepper to taste
¾ cup Marsala or sherry
wine

Sauté onion in butter or butter-and-oil mixture in electric skillet or Dutch oven over low heat for 3 minutes or until soft. **Add** chicken and **brown** on all sides (about 12 to 15 minutes). **Add** mushrooms. **Sprinkle** with nutmeg, salt and pepper. **Add** wine and **simmer** 45 minutes or until chicken is tender. May be prepared well in advance and frozen. Serves 3–4.

VARIATIONS: Young turkey or capon can also be prepared in this manner, but require a slightly longer cooking period.

Serving suggestion: Makes an excellent buffet dish. Keep warm in chafing dish. May be served with boiled potatoes or cooked noodles.

Cook's Notes:

Lamb

BRAISED LAMB

Agnello

6 lamb neck slices (about 2
  lbs.), ½ inch thick
2 tablespoons butter
1 cup onion, sliced (about 1
  large onion)
2 teaspoons celery, chopped
1 4-oz. can whole
  mushrooms, undrained

1½ teaspoons salt or to
  taste
¼ teaspoon pepper or to
  taste
⅛ teaspoon rosemary
  (optional)
2 cups hot cooked rice (½
  cup uncooked)

Melt butter in heavy skillet. **Brown** lamb neck slices on both sides over medium heat (about 10 minutes). **Add** onion and celery. **Cook** 5 minutes longer, stirring occasionally. **Add** mushrooms. **Sprinkle** with salt, pepper and rosemary. **Cover** tightly and reduce heat. **Simmer** 30 minutes or until meat is tender. Spread rice on platter and arrange braised lamb on top of rice. Serve hot. Can be prepared in advance and stored in refrigerator or frozen. Serves 3–4.

VARIATION: **Blend** 1 tablespoon tomato paste with ½ cup warm water. **Add** with mushrooms. **Substitute** ⅛ teaspoon of basil for rosemary.

Cook's Notes:

LAMB SHANKS

Osso di Agnello

4 lamb shanks, about 1½–2
  lbs.
1 clove garlic, quartered
¼ cup flour
2 teaspoons salt
⅛ teaspoon pepper
1 tablespoon butter

1 tablespoon oil
1 cup sliced onion (1
  large onion)
½ lb. fresh mushrooms,
  sliced
2 cups beef bouillon or
  water
¼ cup sherry wine
  (optional)
¼ teaspoon dried oregano

With a sharp knife, make a **slit** in meaty part of lamb shanks
and insert piece of garlic into each slit. **Combine** flour, salt and
pepper on sheet of wax paper. **Heat** butter and oil in Dutch
oven or electric frying pan. **Coat** shanks in seasoned flour and
brown slowly in hot oil on all sides (about 15 to 20 minutes).
Remove shanks and set aside. **Sauté** onions and mushrooms 5
minutes or until onions are transparent, stirring frequently.
Drain off some of excess fat. **Add** shanks and remaining ingredients. **Cover** and **cook** slowly 1 to 1¼ hours or until tender.
May be prepared in advance and frozen. Allow 4 shanks per
serving.

NOTE: If more convenient, transfer browned shanks to 3 qt.
casserole and bake at 300° for 1½ to 2 hours.

Serving suggestion: Serve with hot cooked rice or boiled potatoes.

Cook's Notes:

LAMB WITH SQUASH

Agnello con Cucuzza

2 lbs. boneless lamb
shoulder, cut into 2-inch
cubes
3 tablespoons oil
2 medium onions, sliced
2 fresh tomatoes, peeled and
finely chopped

4 fresh basil leaves or 1
teaspoon dried basil
1 teaspoon salt
¼ teaspoon pepper
1 cucuzza squash (about
1½–2 lbs.)

Heat oil in heavy kettle or Dutch oven over medium heat. **Brown** meat on all sides (about 15 minutes), turning occasionally. **Add** onions and cook 5 minutes longer. **Add** tomatoes and basil; season with salt and pepper. **Cover** tightly and reduce heat. **Simmer** 20 minutes.

Meanwhile, **scrape** cucuzza and cut into 1-inch cubes. **Add** to meat. **Cover and cook** 10 minutes longer or until meat and cucuzza are tender. Preparing well in advance enhances flavor. May be frozen. Serves 6.

NOTE: Cucuzza is a long, pale green summer squash with soft, edible seeds. These squash vary from 12 to 40 inches in length. The smaller the squash, the more tender it will be. Fresh tomatoes improve the flavor of this dish. They may be puréed in a blender instead of chopped.

Serving suggestion: Serve hot with crusty Italian bread.

Cook's Notes:

LAMB VENETIAN STYLE

Agnello alla Veneziana

4 shoulder lamb chops, about ½-inch thick
2 tablespoons butter or margarine
2 medium onions, sliced
1 teaspoon dry mint or 1

tablespoon fresh mint, chopped
Salt and pepper to taste
1 ✕2 can (2½ cups) peas, undrained

Heat butter or margarine in heavy skillet or Dutch oven. **Brown** chops on both sides (7 to 8 minutes), over medium heat. If necessary, **pour off** excess fat. **Add** onion, mint, salt and pepper. **Reduce** heat and **simmer** about 20 minutes or until tender. **Add** undrained peas and **cook** until peas are hot (about 7 to 10 minutes). Serve hot. Serves 4.

NOTE: 2 lbs. lamb stew meat may be substituted for lamb chops.

Serving suggestion: Serve with boiled potatoes or hot cooked rice.

Cook's Notes:

Pork

BREADED PORK CHOPS

Costatelle di Maiale

6 pork chops, about 1 inch
    thick
1 cup bread crumbs
¾ cup Parmesan or
    Romano cheese, grated
Salt and pepper to taste

2 green onion tops, finely
    chopped (optional)
2 eggs, well beaten
2 tablespoons butter
2 tablespoons oil

Trim fat from pork chops. Mix bread crumbs, cheese, salt, pepper and onions in bowl. Dip chops in beaten eggs and then in seasoned crumbs.

Heat oil and butter in skillet with oven-proof handle. Brown chops on one side about 8 minutes over low heat; turn and brown other side. Bake at 350° about 30 minutes or until chops are tender and meat is no longer pink. Serves 6.

NOTE: Pork or veal steaks may be prepared in the same manner.

VARIATION: Marinate pork chops in 1 cup vinegar for 1 hour. Wipe chops with paper towels. Otherwise proceed in the same manner.

Cook's Notes:

PORK CHOPS AND CABBAGE

Costatelle di Maiale con Cavolo

8 pork chops, about ½
  inch thick
¼ cup olive oil
2 medium onions, sliced
1 clove garlic, chopped
2½ cups tomatoes (20 oz.
  can)

1 head cabbage (about 2
  lbs.), coarsely shredded
1 teaspoon salt
⅛ teaspoon pepper
⅛ teaspoon sage
1 cup dry red wine

Heat oil over medium heat in large skillet. **Brown** chops 3
minutes on each side. **Remove** to casserole. In same skillet, **sauté**
onions and garlic 3 minutes. **Stir in** tomatoes, add cabbage and
remaining ingredients. **Spread** over chops. **Bake** at 350° for 60
minutes or until cabbage and chops are tender. Check occasionally. Can be prepared in advance and refrigerated. (If refrigerated, allow 15 minutes additional baking time.) Serves
4–6.

Cook's Notes:

PORK GENOA STYLE

Maiale alla Genovese

4 pork chops, ¾ inch
   thick (about 1½ lbs.)
2 tablespoons oil
Salt and pepper to taste
½ cup water
2 tablespoons white wine
   (optional)

¼ teaspoon basil
1 tablespoon parsley
1 clove garlic, minced
4 small potatoes, peeled and
   cut in halves
4 small carrots
Salt and pepper to taste

Heat oil in skillet with oven-proof handle. **Season** chops with salt and pepper. **Brown** chops on both sides over low heat (about 10 to 12 minutes). **Remove** chops from skillet and **pour off** excess fat. **Combine** water, wine, basil, parsley and garlic in skillet. **Add** potatoes and carrots; sprinkle lightly with salt and pepper. **Return** browned chops to skillet. **Bake** at 350° for 45 to 60 minutes or until potatoes and carrots are tender. Skim off excess fat and serve hot in skillet. Serves 3–4.

VARIATION: **Substitute** 1 cup tomatoes for water.

Cook's Notes:

ITALIAN SAUSAGE CASSEROLE

Casseruola di Salsiccia

2 lbs. sweet Italian sausage
6 medium potatoes, peeled
  and sliced
1 tablespoon onion, minced
1 teaspoon salt
⅛ teaspoon pepper

1 tablespoon butter, melted
1 10½-oz. can condensed
  cream of mushroom soup
1 4-oz. can mushrooms,
  undrained
1 cup water

Place Italian sausage and potatoes in greased 2-qt. casserole.
Combine remaining ingredients in a bowl and **stir** until blended.
Pour over sausage and potatoes. **Bake** in preheated oven at 350°
for 1 hour. Serves 4–6.

Cook's Notes:

MARINATED PORK CHOPS

Costatelle di Maiale

4 loin or rib pork chops, 1
  inch thick
1 cup wine vinegar
1 clove garlic, minced
1 small onion, chopped
2 eggs
1½ cups bread crumbs

2 tablespoons Romano
  cheese, grated
2 tablespoons parsley,
  chopped
Salt and pepper to taste
½ cup flour
4 tablespoons olive oil

In glass bowl **combine** vinegar, garlic and onion. Add chops
and **marinate** for 1 hour. **Drain** chops and wipe with paper
towels. **Beat** eggs. **Combine** bread crumbs, cheese, parsley, salt
and pepper in bowl. **Dredge** chops in flour; dip in eggs, then in
seasoned crumbs. **Grease** casserole with 2 tablespoons oil, and
arrange chops in casserole. **Drizzle** balance of oil over chops and
cover. **Bake** at 350° for 1 hour or until tender. Check occasionally; if pan becomes dry, drizzle 2 tablespoons water over
chops. Can be prepared in advance, stored in refrigerator and
baked later. Serves 4.

VARIATION: Substitute 2 lbs. 1 inch thick round steak, cut
into serving pieces, for pork chops.

Serving suggestion: Serve with small new boiled potatoes and
sliced fresh tomatoes.

Cook's Notes:

PORK CHOPS WITH VERMOUTH

Costatelle di Maiale con Vino

6 rib pork chops, ¾ inch
thick (about 3 lbs.)
2 tablespoons butter or
margarine
2 tablespoons oil
1 cup rice, uncooked
1 large onion, sliced
2 stalks celery, cut
diagonally every two
inches
1 can (1 lb.) tomatoes,
strained or whirled in
blender

1 cup dry vermouth
1½ teaspoons salt
⅛ teaspoon pepper
¼ teaspoon crushed
rosemary or sage
(optional)
2 tablespoons Parmesan or
Romano cheese, grated
1 green pepper, cut into
rings

Heat butter and oil in skillet over medium heat. **Brown**
chops about 5 minutes on each side. **Spread** rice over bottom of
casserole. **Arrange** browned chops on top. **Add** onion and celery
to skillet drippings. **Sauté** 5 minutes, stirring occasionally. **Add**
tomatoes, wine, salt, pepper and rosemary. **Pour** mixture **over**
chops. **Sprinkle** with cheese and **top** with green pepper rings.
Cover and **bake** at 350° for 1¼ hours or until chops and rice
are tender. Can be prepared in advance and refrigerated or
frozen. (If refrigerated, bake 1½ hours.) Serves 6.

Cook's Notes:

SPARERIBS FRIULI

Costole alla Friuli

3 lbs. spareribs, cut into
2-inch pieces
1–2 tablespoons oil
(depending on amount of
fat in spareribs)
3 stalks celery with tops,
chopped
2 cloves garlic

2 medium carrots, chopped
1½ teaspoons salt or to
taste
⅛ teaspoon pepper
2 cups water
½ teaspoon sage
1 medium head of green
cabbage, cut into 2-inch
wide wedges

Heat oil in electric frying pan or Dutch oven over medium heat, and sauté spareribs until brown on all sides (about 10 minutes), turning often. Reduce heat. Add celery, celery tops, garlic and carrots. Sprinkle with salt and pepper. Sauté 5 minutes, turning occasionally. Discard garlic. Add water and sage. Cover and simmer 1 hour. Add cabbage and cook 10 minutes or until cabbage is tender but not mushy. Can be frozen for later use. Serves 6.

NOTE: Pork neck bones or pigs' knuckles may be substituted for ribs; cook 2 hours instead of 1 hour and add 2 cups of water.

VARIATION: *With Beans*
Omit cabbage. Sauté 1 lb. whole green beans with vegetables. Add 1 cup tomato juice. Substitute ¼ teaspoon thyme for sage.

Cook's Notes:

Veal

VEAL CASSEROLE

Casseruola di Vitello

2 lb. veal rump, cut into
  1½ inch cubes
6 tablespoons flour
2 teaspoons salt
⅛ teaspoon pepper
6 tablespoons butter
4 medium onions, sliced
¼ cup parsley

½ lb. fresh mushrooms,
  sliced
1 stalk celery, chopped
1 medium carrot, chopped
1 tablespoon tomato paste
2 chicken bouillon cubes,
  dissolved in 2 cups
  boiling water
½ cup dry white wine

Combine flour, salt and pepper. **Coat** meat with flour mixture. **Melt** butter in skillet and **brown** veal 5 minutes, turning occasionally. **Remove** and set aside. In same skillet, **sauté** onions, parsley, mushrooms, celery and carrot for 10 minutes, stirring occasionally to prevent sticking. **Add** remaining ingredients. **Transfer** to casserole or Dutch oven. **Add** browned veal. **Cover and cook** over low heat 1¼ hours or until meat and vegetables are tender. Check occasionally. Can be prepared in advance and frozen. Serves 6.

Cook's Notes:

VEAL WITH CHEESE

Costatelle di Vitello con Formaggio

12 very thinly sliced veal
cutlets, cut into 5-inch
squares
12 thin slices prosciutto or
ham
12 thin slices Fontina
cheese
1 cup bread crumbs

¼ cup Parmesan cheese,
grated
1 teaspoon salt
⅛ teaspoon pepper
2 eggs, beaten
4 tablespoons butter
4 tablespoons olive oil

Lay 6 slices of veal on waxed paper. **Top** each slice with 2
slices of prosciutto and 2 slices of Fontina cheese. **Cover** with
remaining veal slices to form sandwiches. Pat edges together and
fasten with skewers or toothpicks. **Combine** bread crumbs, grated
cheese, salt and pepper. **Dip** sandwiches in eggs and then in
seasoned bread crumbs. **Heat** butter and oil in skillet over medium heat. **Brown** sandwiches 3 minutes on each side. Lift
gently from skillet. **Place** on ovenproof platter or in oblong casserole. **Bake** in 350° oven for 10 minutes or until cheese melts.
Serves 6.

Serving suggestion: Serve with mixed green salad.

Cook's Notes:

CHOPS CASSEROLE

Costatelle Pasticcio

2½ lbs. (about 8) veal,
  pork or lamb shoulder
  chops
¼ cup flour
½ teaspoon salt
⅛ teaspoon pepper
2 tablespoons butter
2 tablespoons olive oil
½ cup dry white wine
1 bouillon cube, dissolved in
  1 cup hot water
4 medium potatoes, peeled

and sliced ½ inch thick
Salt and pepper to taste
1 lb. fresh mushrooms,
  washed and sliced
2 medium onions, sliced in
  thin rings
1 clove garlic, minced
2 tablespoons parsley
  chopped
¼ teaspoon rosemary,
  crushed

Combine flour, salt and pepper in bowl. **Dust** chops with flour. **Heat** butter and oil in frying pan over medium heat. **Brown** chops 5 minutes on each side, adding more oil if necessary. **Remove** when browned. In same pan, **add** wine and bouillon. **Bring to boil**, stirring to loosen browned bits. Set aside. **Place** potatoes on bottom of casserole. **Sprinkle** with salt and pepper. **Arrange** mushrooms and onions over potatoes. **Top** with chops. **Pour** wine mixture over all. **Sprinkle** with garlic, parsley and rosemary. **Cover and bake** at 350° for 1¼ hours or until chops and vegetables are tender. Check occasionally. Serve from casserole. Can be assembled one day ahead and refrigerated until ready to use. If refrigerated, allow 15 or 20 minutes extra baking time. Serves 4–6.

Cook's Notes:

CORNMEAL WITH VEAL

Polenta con Vitello

2 lbs. boneless veal, cut
    into 1½-inch cubes
2 tablespoons olive oil
2 tablespoons lard
1 clove garlic
¼ cup green onion tops or
    onion
1 29-oz. can tomatoes

1½ teaspoons salt
⅛ teaspoon pepper
½ teaspoon dried basil or
    6 fresh leaves, chopped
1 cup cornmeal
2 tablespoons Parmesan
    cheese, grated (optional)

Heat oil and lard in skillet. **Brown** meat over medium heat 10 minutes, turning frequently. **Push aside** meat and **sauté** garlic and onion for 3 minutes; stir. **Strain** tomatoes or put through blender. **Add** to meat. **Season** with salt and pepper; **add** basil. Bring to boil. **Reduce** heat and **cook** for 30 to 45 minutes or until meat is tender. Check seasoning. **Cook** cornmeal according to label on package. Place on platter and top with sauce and meat. If desired, sprinkle with Parmesan cheese. Serves 4.

Cook's Notes:

VEAL MESSINA STYLE

Vitello alla Messinese

1½ lbs. veal rump, cut into 1½-inch pieces
2 tablespoons oil
1 clove garlic
1 small onion, chopped
½ lb. string beans (or peas)
1 large fresh ripe tomato
1 medium carrot
1 stalk celery, chopped
⅛ teaspoon basil or 2 fresh basil leaves
⅛ teaspoon oregano
½ bay leaf
1 cup water
Salt and pepper to taste
3 medium potatoes, peeled and quartered

Heat oil in Dutch oven or heavy skillet. **Add** meat and brown over low heat on all sides (about 10 minutes); turn meat frequently for even browning. During last minute of browning **add** garlic and onion.

Meanwhile, **wash and prepare** vegetables. Remove ends of string beans; leave whole or cut into halves. Plunge tomato in boiling water for 1 minute; peel and put into blender. Scrape carrot and cut into 1-inch pieces. After meat has browned **add** all remaining ingredients except potatoes. **Stir and cover. Reduce** heat to low and **cook** 45 minutes. Stir from time to time, adding 2 tablespoons water if necessary. **Add** potatoes and cook 20 minutes longer, or until meat and vegetables are tender. Preparing well in advance improves flavor. May be frozen, omitting potatoes and bay leaf.

Cook's Notes:

VEAL WITH MUSHROOMS AND CHEESE

Vitello con Funghi e Formaggio

2 lbs. veal steak, cut into
  serving pieces
2 cups bread crumbs
Salt and pepper to taste
¼ teaspoon dried basil
  or 1 tablespoon fresh
  basil, chopped
¼ cup Parmesan or
  Romano cheese, grated

2 eggs, slightly beaten
4 tablespoons oil
3 cups tomato sauce
Sautéed mushrooms (recipe
  below)
2 6-oz. packages Provolone
  cheese, sliced

In large bowl, **combine** bread crumbs, salt, pepper, basil and cheese. **Dip** meat slices in beaten eggs, then in seasoned crumbs. **Heat** oil in heavy skillet and **brown** meat on one side for about 5 minutes over medium heat; turn and brown on other side for 3 minutes. Add more oil if needed during browning process. **Remove** meat and set aside. **Spread** thin layer of tomato sauce over bottom of baking pan; **add** layer of meat, then layer of sautéed mushrooms. **Top** with Provolone slices. **Cover** with ⅓ of sauce. **Repeat** until all ingredients are used up, ending with sauce. **Bake** in preheated oven at 350° about 1¼ hours or until meat is tender. Check occasionally, adding more sauce or water if necessary. Serve hot. If prepared in advance, increase baking time 15 to 20 minutes. Serves 6.

Sautéed Mushroom

2 tablespoons olive oil
2 medium onions, thinly
  sliced

1 lb. fresh mushrooms,
  cleaned and sliced

Heat oil in skillet over medium heat. **Add** onions and **sauté** 2 minutes, stirring constantly. **Add** mushrooms and **sauté** 3 minutes longer, stirring occasionally. Set aside until ready to use.

VARIATION: **Substitute** 2 pounds eye of rib steak or round steak for veal steak.

Cook's Notes:

VEAL WITH PEPPERS AND POTATOES

Vitello con Peperoni e Patate

4 veal chops (½ inch thick)   4 medium green peppers,
6 tablespoons olive oil   cut into 1-inch strips
1 clove garlic   4 medium potatoes, sliced
2 small onions, sliced   Salt and pepper to taste

Heat oil in skillet over medium heat. **Brown** garlic 2 minutes
and discard. **Brown** chops 5 minutes on each side; set aside.
Sauté onions, peppers and potatoes for 5 minutes, turning frequently to prevent sticking. **Transfer** vegetables to casserole. **Top**
with chops. **Season** with salt and pepper. **Cover and bake** at
375° for 30 minutes or until meat and vegetables are done.
Serves 4.

Cook's Notes:

VEAL ROLLS

Rotoli di Vitello

12 thin veal scallops (about 2 lbs.), cut into 4-inch squares
Salt and pepper to taste
12 sticks (about ¼ lb.) Fontina cheese
12 thin slices prosciutto or cooked ham

12 sage leaves
¼ cup butter
⅓ cup dry white wine
½ lb. hot boiled egg noodles, buttered

Season each veal scallop with salt and pepper. On each slice **place** cheese stick, prosciutto and sage leaf. **Roll up** each scallop; tie with thread or secure with small skewers. **Melt** butter over medium heat in skillet. **Brown** meat rolls on all sides about 6 to 8 minutes or until golden brown, turning frequently. **Place** in heated serving dish or chafing dish. **Remove** thread or skewers. **Stir** wine into skillet, scraping the bottom. **Bring** to boil. **Pour** over rolls. Serve with noodles. Serves 6.

Cook's Notes:

LAYERED SALTIMBOCCA

Saltimbocca

8 thinly sliced veal cutlets,
  cut into 4-inch squares
2 tablespoons butter
2 tablespoons oil
¼ teaspoon sage
Salt and pepper to taste

8 thin slices prosciutto or
  boiled ham
8 thin slices Provolone or
  mozzarella cheese
¼ cup water

Heat butter and oil in skillet with oven-proof handle. **Brown** cutlets over medium heat ½ minute on each side. **Sprinkle** with sage, salt and pepper. **Place** a slice of prosciutto on each cutlet and **top** with a slice of cheese. **Bake** at 375° for 4 minutes or until cheese melts. Transfer to warmed serving dish with cheese side up. **Pour** water into skillet; scrape up bottom of skillet. **Simmer** for 1 to 2 minutes. **Pour** over saltimbocca. Serves 4.

Serving suggestion: Serve with hot cooked rice and peas.

Cook's Notes:

VEAL SHANKS WITH NOODLES

Osso Buco con Fettucine

4 meaty veal shanks with
  marrow in center, sawed
  crosswise into 2-inch
  pieces
2 tablespoons flour
1 teaspoon salt
⅛ teaspoon pepper
¼ cup butter
1 medium onion, minced
1 clove garlic, minced
1 carrot, grated
½ cup diced celery
2 tablespoons tomato purée

or 1 medium tomato,
  peeled and diced
1 cup soup stock, bouillon
  or water
1 cup white wine
4 strips lemon peel, 1 inch
  long
2 tablespoons parsley,
  snipped
½ lb. hot cooked green
  noodles or egg noodles

Put flour, salt and pepper into paper bag; drop veal shanks into flour mixture and shake bag enough to dredge veal shanks. **Melt** butter in Dutch oven or electric skillet and **brown** veal on both sides over medium heat (about 5 to 6 minutes). **Remove** shanks as they brown and set aside. **Add** onion, garlic, carrot and celery to Dutch oven or electric skillet. **Sauté,** stirring constantly, about 5 minutes or until tender. **Return** meat to Dutch oven or electric skillet. **Add** all remaining ingredients except parsley and noodles. **Stir** well. **Cover** and **simmer** 1 hour or until meat is tender, stirring constantly; add teaspoon soup, water or wine if needed. Taste to correct seasoning. Just before serving **stir in** parsley. Meanwhile **cook** noodles according to instructions on package. **Remove** shanks to platter; surround with noodles. **Pour** sauce over noodles. Can be prepared in advance or frozen. Do not cook noodles until ready to serve. Serves 4.

VEAL WITH POTATOES

Vitello con Patate

2 lbs. arm or round veal
steak, ½ inch thick, cut
into serving pieces
1½ cups bread crumbs
¼ cup Romano or
Parmesan cheese, grated
1 tablespoon onion, minced
1 tablespoon parsley,
chopped

⅛ teaspoon pepper
½ teaspoon salt or to taste
½ cup oil
4 medium potatoes, peeled
and sliced lengthwise, ¼
inch thick
2 tablespoons oil
2 tablespoons lard

In a bowl, **combine** bread crumbs, cheese, onion, parsley, pepper and salt. **Mix** thoroughly. **Dip** veal steaks in oil, then into bread crumbs. With 2 tablespoons oil, **grease** bottom of 12×8×2 inch baking dish or 3-qt. casserole. **Alternate** layers of breaded meat and potatoes. **Dot** with lard. **Bake** uncovered in preheated oven at 350° for 45 to 60 minutes or until potatoes are tender. Check after 45 minutes. Serves 4–5.

Cook's Notes:

VEAL ROMAN STYLE

Vitello alla Romana

2 lbs. boneless veal, cut into
  1-inch cubes
¼ cup butter
1 medium onion, minced
2 stalks celery, sliced into
  1-inch pieces

½ lb. fresh mushrooms,
  sliced
¼ teaspoon rosemary
1 teaspoon salt or to taste
1 cup white wine or chicken
  broth

Melt butter in oven-proof skillet or 2-qt. casserole. **Add** meat and **brown** on all sides over low heat 10 minutes, turning frequently. **Add** vegetables and sauté 5 minutes. **Sprinkle** with rosemary, salt, pepper, and wine or chicken broth. **Cover** and **bake** at 350° for 1 hour or until meat and vegetables are tender, stirring occasionally. May be frozen indefinitely. Serves 4–6.

NOTE: May be cooked on top of stove or in electric skillet.

Serving suggestion: Serve with hot boiled potatoes. Makes an excellent buffet dish.

Cook's Notes:

VEAL SHANKS

Osso Buco

4 (about 4–6 lbs.) meaty
  veal shanks with marrow
  in center, sawed crosswise
  into 2-inch pieces
½ cup flour
1 teaspoon salt
⅛ teaspoon pepper
4 tablespoons butter

2 cups chicken broth
  (canned or homemade) or
  water
1 cup dry white wine
2 tablespoons parsley,
  chopped
1 clove garlic, minced
Grated rind of 1 lemon
4 cups hot risotto or rice

Put flour, salt and pepper into paper bag. Drop veal shanks a few at a time into flour mixture. Shake well to coat. Melt butter in Dutch oven or large heavy pan. Brown shanks on all sides over medium heat 10 minutes or until well browned. Do not crowd. Remove shanks as they brown. Add more butter if needed during browning process. Return browned shanks to Dutch oven or heavy pan. Arrange shanks in one or two layers, so marrow in bones does not fall out as they cook. Add broth or water and wine. Cover tightly and cook over low fire about 1½ hours or until meat is tender. Check occasionally, adding more broth or water if necessary. Taste for seasoning, adding salt and pepper if needed. Recipe can be prepared in advance up to this point. Cool and store in refrigerator or in freezer. To serve, sprinkle with parsley, garlic and lemon rind. Cook five minutes longer. Remove veal shanks to platter or individual plates. Surround with rice. Pour some sauce over rice and serve remaining sauce separately. Serves 4–6.

Cook's Notes:

Seafood and Fish

CRAB FLORENTINE STYLE

Granchi alla Fiorentina

2 cups or 2 6½-oz. cans
  crab meat
1 cup water
2 lbs. fresh spinach, washed
  and chopped, or 2 10-oz.
  frozen packages
1 cup (¼ lb.) Provolone
  cheese, shredded
½ cup onion, finely chopped

2 tablespoons butter
2 tablespoons flour
1 cup milk
¼ cup dry white wine
  (optional)
¼ teaspoon salt
⅛ teaspoon pepper
1 tablespoon lemon juice

Boil water. **Put** in spinach, and **cook** 2 minutes. **Drain. Arrange** spinach in bottom of 1½ qt. casserole. **Sprinkle** with ½ cup shredded Provolone. **Set** aside. **Cook** butter and onion in saucepan for 2 minutes. **Blend** in flour. **Add** milk, wine, salt and pepper. **Bring** to boil; stir 1 minute. **Cook** 2 minutes longer, stirring constantly to prevent lumps. **Remove** from heat. **Stir** in remaining ½ cup Provolone, crab meat and lemon juice. **Spread** mixture over spinach. **Bake** at 375° for 20 minutes or until bubbly. Can be prepared in advance and refrigerated. (If refrigerated, allow 15 minutes more for baking.) Serves 6.

Cook's Notes:

LOBSTER FRA DIAVOLO

Aragosta fra Diavolo

2 medium lobsters (about
  1–1½ lbs.)
¼ cup olive oil
2 cloves garlic, chopped
1 16-oz. can tomatoes (2
  cups)
1 teaspoon oregano

1 tablespoon parsley,
  chopped
½ teaspoon salt
¼ teaspoon crushed red
  pepper seeds
½ cup dry white wine

Split lobsters in half lengthwise. **Remove** intestinal veins and head sacs; discard. **Place** lobsters, cut side up, in casserole. **Set** aside. **Heat** oil in skillet. **Sauté** garlic for 2 minutes. **Add** tomatoes, crushing whole tomatoes with fork. **Stir in** remaining ingredients. **Simmer** 10 minutes, stirring occasionally. Pour evenly over lobster. Bake at 400° for 20 minutes or until lobster is cooked. Serves 2–4.

Serving suggestion: Serve with ½ lb. cooked and drained spaghettini. Spoon sauce over spaghettini.

Cook's Notes:

MUSSELS OR CLAMS

Mitili

3 dozen fresh mussels or clams with tightly closed shells
¼ cup olive oil or 2 tablespoons oil and 2 tablespoons butter
1 clove garlic, minced
2 tablespoons parsley, minced

2 tablespoons butter
1 medium onion, chopped
1 cup uncooked rice
1½ cups water (approx.)
2 tablespoons sherry wine (optional)
Salt and pepper to taste
¼ cup Parmesan cheese, grated (optional)

Scrub mussels or clams well with vegetable brush, and scrape with knife. **Heat** oil or butter in large deep kettle. **Add** garlic, parsley, and mussels or clams. **Cover** and **steam** 3 minutes or until shells open. **Discard** shells. **Strain** liquid and reserve. Set **aside** mussel or clam meat. **Melt** 2 tablespoons butter in casserole or saucepan over medium heat. **Sauté** onion 2 minutes or until soft. **Add** rice, stirring steadily until rice is coated with butter. **Add** water, wine and reserved mussel or clam liquid. **Season** with salt and pepper. **Reduce** heat and **simmer** 14 to 18 minutes or until rice is tender but still firm. **Add** mussels or clams and grated cheese if desired. **Cook** 3 minutes; stirring if necessary. **Add** more water. Rice should be moist but not soupy. Can be prepared ahead of time; may be frozen. 4 generous servings.

Serving suggestion: Serve with crusty Italian bread.

Cook's Notes:

SCALLOPS CASSEROLE

Casseruola di Scampi

1 lb. scallops fresh or
 frozen, cut into halves
1/4 cup olive oil
2 medium onions, chopped
1 medium green pepper,
 chopped
1/2 cup celery, chopped
1/2 lb. fresh mushrooms,
 sliced

1 1 lb., 12-oz. (3 1/2 cups)
 can tomatoes, mashed
1/4 teaspoon oregano
1 teaspoon salt
1/8 teaspoon pepper
1/4 cup dry red wine
4 cups cooked rice (1 1/4
 cups raw)

Thaw scallops if frozen. Heat oil in skillet over medium fire.
Sauté scallops 5 minutes, turning occasionally. Remove and set
aside. In same skillet, add onions, green pepper, celery and
mushrooms. Cook 5 minutes, stirring occasionally. Add tomatoes,
oregano, salt, pepper and wine. Bring to boil and add scallops.
Cook 15 minutes. Remove from heat. Taste, add more salt and
pepper if needed. Place rice in 2 qt. casserole. Pour scallop sauce
over. Bake at 350° for 20 minutes or until bubbly. Can be prepared in advance and refrigerated. (If refrigerated, allow 15
minutes more for baking.) Serves 4.

Cook's Notes:

SHRIMP WITH WINE

Gamberi con Vino

1 lb. shrimp	½ lb. fresh mushrooms,
1 tablespoon butter	sliced
1 tablespoon olive oil	¼ cup sherry or any white
6 green onions including	wine
tops, finely chopped	Salt and pepper to taste

Shell and de-vein shrimp (remove dark vein from center back); set aside. **Melt** butter in skillet over medium fire. **Add** oil and **sauté** onions 2 minutes over low fire. **Add** mushrooms and **sauté** 5 minutes, stirring occasionally. **Add** wine, salt and pepper. **Bring to** a boiling point; then **add** shrimp. **Simmer** until shrimp become pink (about 4 minutes for medium, 5 minutes for large). Can be frozen. Serves 4.

Serving suggestion: Serve with hot cooked rice. Excellent for a buffet. Recipe can be easily doubled.

Cook's Notes:

FISH STEAK WITH POTATOES

Pesce con Patate

4 thick halibut steaks
  (about 2 lbs.)
4 medium potatoes, peeled
  and quartered
2 medium onions, sliced
½ cup olive oil
1 1-lb. can tomatoes

1 cup dry white wine or
  water
2 tablespoons parsley,
  chopped
½ teaspoon oregano
1 teaspoon salt
¼ teaspoon freshly ground
  pepper

Place fish steaks in casserole or deep baking pan. **Arrange** potatoes and onions around fish. **Pour** oil over fish and vegetables. **Add** tomatoes, crushing with fingers. **Spread** over fish. **Pour** wine. **Combine** parsley and oregano. **Sprinkle** over all. **Season** with salt and pepper. **Bake** at 350° for 35 to 45 minutes or until fish and vegetables are tender. Serves 4.

Cook's Notes:

TUNA CALABRIAN STYLE

Tonno alla Calabrese

2 lbs. fresh tuna, sliced
½ inch thick
½ cup oil
3 medium onions, thinly
sliced
4 medium green peppers,
cut into 1-inch strips

8 medium (2 lbs.) ripe
tomatoes, peeled and
chopped
6 fresh basil leaves
1 teaspoon salt
¼ teaspoon crushed red
pepper seeds

Heat oil in skillet over medium heat. Brown fish 5 minutes on each side. Remove fish and transfer to casserole or Dutch oven. In same skillet add onions and green peppers and sauté 5 minutes, turning occasionally. Add tomatoes, basil, salt and pepper seeds. Cover and cook 10 minutes, stirring occasionally. Remove from heat, and pour over tuna. Cover casserole or Dutch oven. Cook 15 minutes or until fish flakes easily with fork. Taste and add salt if needed. Preparing this dish a day ahead of time and reheating will improve flavor. Can be frozen. Serves 4–6.

Serving suggestion: Serve with tossed green salad and crusty Italian bread.

Cook's Notes:

TUNA MARCHES STYLE

Tonna alla Marche

2 lbs. fresh tuna, sliced 1-
inch thick
2 tablespoons olive oil
1 onion, chopped
3 tablespoons tomato paste
1½ cups water
½ cup dry white wine
¼ teaspoon basil
2 lbs. fresh peas, shelled
or 2 10-oz. packages
frozen, thawed

½ cup flour
1 teaspoon salt
¼ teaspoon freshly ground
pepper
¼ cup olive oil
12 (about 2 lbs.) small new
potatoes, cooked and
peeled
½ cup parsley, chopped

Heat 2 tablespoons oil in casserole or Dutch oven. **Sauté** onion
2 minutes. **Stir** in tomato paste, water and wine. **Bring to** boil.
Boil 5 minutes. **Add** peas. **Cook** 5 minutes longer. While peas are
cooking, **combine** flour, salt and pepper in bowl. **Dredge** tuna in
seasoned flour. **Heat** ¼ cup oil in skillet over medium fire.
Brown tuna 5 minutes on each side. **Remove** carefully. **Add** to
boiling pea sauce. **Cover** and cook 15 to 20 minutes or until fish
flakes easily with fork. **Taste** for seasoning. **Remove** tuna carefully
to platter. **Arrange** potatoes around tuna. **Pour** pea sauce over
fish and potatoes. **Sprinkle** with parsley. Can be prepared a day
ahead and refrigerated. (If refrigerated, omit potatoes until
ready to serve.) Serves 6.

Cook's Notes:

FISH VENETIAN STYLE

Pesce alla Veneziana

2 pounds sole or haddock
filets
6 tablespoons butter
1 small onion, minced
½ lb. fresh mushrooms,
sliced

¼ cup parsley, minced
1 teaspoon salt
⅛ teaspoon pepper
¼ teaspoon thyme

Melt butter in casserole. Sauté onion, mushrooms and parsley
5 minutes, stirring often. Stir in salt, pepper, and thyme. Add fish,
and lower heat. Cover and cook 10 minutes. Turn filets and
cook 10 minutes longer or until fish flakes easily with fork.
Serves 6.

Cook's Notes:

WHITING WITH WINE

Merluzzo con Vino

2 lbs. whitings, cleaned and
   split
1 tablespoon butter
2 medium onions, thinly
   sliced
½ lb. fresh mushrooms,
   sliced
1 teaspoon salt
¼ teaspoon pepper

2 tablespoons bread crumbs
1 tablespoon Parmesan
   cheese, grated
¼ teaspoon sage
¼ cup butter, melted
½ cup dry white wine
Juice of ½ lemon

Grease casserole or baking pan with 1 tablespoon butter.
Arrange onions in bottom of casserole. **Top** with mushrooms.
Place whitings skin side up. **Sprinkle** with salt, pepper, crumbs,
cheese and sage. **Pour** melted butter and wine over fish. **Bake** at
400° for 20 minutes or until fish flakes easily with fork. **Remove**
from oven and **drizzle** with lemon juice. Serves 4.

Cook's Notes:

SARDINES WITH FENNEL

Sarde con Finocchio

2 lbs. fresh sardines, cleaned, boned and split	1 6-oz. can tomato paste
½ cup olive oil	2 cups water
2 cloves garlic	1 tablespoon seedless raisins
1 fresh fennel with leaves (about 1 lb.), washed and chopped	1 tablespoon pine nuts
	Salt and pepper to taste
	1 tablespoon olive oil
1 quart boiling water	2 cups bread crumbs
	1 lb. spaghetti or bucatini

Heat oil in skillet over medium fire. Lay sardines skin side down. Sauté 10 minutes. Remove to dish with pancake turner. In same skillet, sauté garlic 2 minutes. Set skillet aside. Meanwhile, cook fennel in boiling water 5 minutes. Drain and reserve one cup liquid. Add fennel to garlic and sauté 5 minutes. Stir in tomato paste and 2 cups water. Cook 10 minutes. Add sardines, fennel liquid, raisins, pine nuts, salt and pepper. Cook 30 minutes, stirring occasionally. While fish sauce is cooking, heat one tablespoon oil in skillet over medium fire. Stir in bread crumbs. Toast 8 minutes or until lightly brown, stirring occasionally. Remove until ready to use.

Cook spaghetti according to instructions on package until chewy (al dente). Spread thin layer fish sauce in deep casserole or baking pan. Place layer of spaghetti. Sprinkle with toasted crumbs. Repeat layers until all ingredients are used. Bake at 350° for 20 minutes or until bubbly, but not dry. Fish sauce can be prepared in advance and stored in refrigerator or frozen. Serves 6.

CODFISH NEAPOLITAN STYLE

Baccalá alla Napoletana

1 whole dry codfish (about
  1½–2 lbs.)
Water
½ cup flour
⅛ teaspoon pepper
½ cup olive oil

1 clove garlic, minced
1 tablespoon capers
24 pitted green olives, sliced
2 tablespoons tomato paste
1 cup water

Soak codfish in cold water to cover for 24 hours. **Drain** and **wash** several times in cold water. **Cut** into 3-inch serving pieces. **Combine** flour and pepper in bowl. **Roll** codfish in flour. **Heat** oil in skillet and **brown** fish 3 to 4 minutes on each side. **Remove** and **place** in casserole. **Sprinkle** with garlic, capers and olives. **Stir** tomato paste in water, and **pour** over fish. **Bake** at 375° for 30 minutes or until fish flakes when tested with fork. Taste and add salt if needed. Serves 4.

Cook's Notes:

CODFISH SICILIAN STYLE

Baccalá alla Siciliana

1 whole dry codfish (about
  1½–2 lbs.)
Water
¼ cup olive oil
1 medium onion, minced
1 1-lb. 12-oz. can (3½
  cups) tomatoes

12 oil-cured black olives,
  pitted
1 tablespoon seedless raisins
10 pine nuts
1 tablespoon celery, chopped
1 tablespoon parsley,
  chopped
¼ teaspoon basil
Pepper to taste

Soak codfish in cold water to cover for 24 hours. **Drain**, and
wash several times in cold water. **Cut** into 3-inch pieces, and
set aside. **Heat** oil in casserole or Dutch oven. **Sauté** onions for 3
minutes. **Add** all ingredients except codfish. **Cook** 20 minutes,
stirring occasionally. **Add** codfish and **cook** 30 minutes longer or
until fish is tender. **Taste** and add salt if needed. Preparing this
dish in advance will enhance flavor. Serves 4.

VARIATION: *Codfish with potatoes*

Add to sauce ingredients 3 medium potatoes, peeled and quartered.

Cook's Notes:

FILET OF SOLE

Filetti di Sogliole

2 lbs. sole filets
1 tablespoon butter
2 bay leaves, crushed
½ teaspoon thyme
½ cup dry white wine
¼ cup butter
½ cup scallions or green
  onions, minced
2 tablespoons flour

1 cup thin cream
2 tablespoons parsley,
  chopped
½ teaspoon salt
¼ teaspoon freshly ground
  pepper
2 tablespoons Fontina or
  Romano cheese, grated
Hot cooked small
  potatoes

Grease casserole with 1 tablespoon butter. Place filets in single layer. Sprinkle with bay leaves and thyme. Pour wine over filets, and set aside. Melt butter in saucepan. Add scallions; stir 2 minutes. Stir in flour and stir 1 minute. Add cream and simmer 2 minutes stirring constantly. Turn off heat. Stir in parsley, salt, pepper and cheese. Pour sauce over fish. Bake in preheated oven at 375° for 25 minutes or until fish easily flakes with fork. Serve hot with potatoes. Serves 5–6.

Cook's Notes:

Pasta

BOW NOODLES CASSEROLE

Farfalle

¼ cup butter
¼ lb. fresh mushrooms, sliced
2 cups cooked chicken or turkey, diced
3 tablespoons butter
3 tablespoons flour
2½ cups chicken broth or 2 10½-oz. cans
½ cup cream

¼ cup Marsala or sherry wine
1 teaspoon salt
⅛ teaspoon pepper
½ lb. Farfalle (large bow noodles), cooked al dente (chewy) and drained
½ cup Parmesan cheese, grated

Melt ¼ cup butter in skillet. **Add** mushrooms. **Sauté** 3 minutes. **Stir in** cooked chicken or turkey. **Cook** 3 minutes longer, stirring occasionally. **Set aside. Cook** butter and flour in saucepan 2 minutes without browning. **Stir in** broth and cream. **Bring to** boil, stirring 1 minute. **Cook** 2 minutes longer, stirring constantly to prevent lumps. **Remove** from heat. **Stir** in wine, salt and pepper. **Place** cooked bow noodles, sautéed mushrooms and chicken in bowl. **Pour** sauce over and **toss** well with two forks. **Place** in casserole and **sprinkle** with cheese. **Bake** at 350° for 15 to 20 minutes or until golden brown. Can be prepared in advance and refrigerated. (If refrigerated, allow 15 minutes more for baking.) Serves 4–6.

NOTE: Excellent company dish. Can be made in chafing dish.

Cook's Notes:

CANNELLONI TUSCANY

Cannelloni alla Toscana

Cannelloni are thick tubes of paste which originated over a century ago in Nice, on the Riviera. At that time, Nice was under Italian rule. Cannelloni are at their best when homemade. The dough is simple enough to make.

To freeze, allow homemade noodles to dry very thoroughly. Place them between sheets of wax paper before freezing.

Dough #1

2 cups sifted flour
2 eggs well beaten
1½ teaspoons oil or butter

1–2 tablespoons lukewarm
  water, if necessary

Dough #2

⅔ cup sifted flour
⅓ cup semolina

2 eggs
2 tablespoons water

Put flour in bowl; make a well in the center. **Place** beaten egg and oil or butter in well. **Mix** flour, oil and eggs together by hand, adding more flour or water if needed to make dough stiff but soft enough to knead. **Put** on board or smooth table, and knead until smooth and elastic. **Place** bowl over dough; let set about 20 minutes to make dough easier to roll. **Divide** into three parts. **Roll** each with rolling pin or noodle machine into sheets about ⅛ inch thick. **Cut** sheets into 4-inch squares. **Cook** 6 squares at a time in 5 quarts boiling water salted with 1 tablespoon salt. **Remove** with slotted spoon. **Drop** in bowl of cold water momentarily. **Drain** on towel. **Repeat** process until all squares are cooked. **Fill** center of each square with 1½ tablespoons filling (see recipe below). **Roll** up like jelly roll. **Press** edges to prevent filling from falling out. **Place** side by side in 2 qt. casserole or 8″×12″×2″ baking pan greased with 1 tablespoon butter. Cover with remaining sauce and **sprinkle** with 4 tablespoons grated Parmesan cheese. **Bake** uncovered at 375° for 20 minutes. Serve hot; pick up one at a time. May be prepared in advance and frozen. Serves 6.

NOTE: Cannelloni may be purchased ready-made. If using factory-produced Cannelloni, **drop** contents of package into boiling salted water for only 5 minutes. Cannelloni dough may also be used to make Manicotti and lasagne. Simply follow directions for Cannelloni.

Filling

⅓ cup (about 6 tablespoons) butter
1 chicken breast, skinned, boned, and cut into chunks

3 chicken livers
4 thin slices prosciutto or cooked ham
½ cup Parmesan cheese, grated

Melt butter in frying pan. **Add** chicken breast and **sauté** 5 minutes over medium fire, stirring frequently. **Add** chicken livers and **sauté** 5 minutes longer, stirring occasionally. **Cool. Put** chicken breast, livers and ham through fine food grinder. **Add** cheese and **mix.** Place in refrigerator until ready to use.

Sauce

2 tablespoons butter
2 tablespoons flour
1½ cups milk
½ cup cream

½ teaspoon salt
⅛ teaspoon pepper
Pinch of nutmeg (optional)

Melt butter in heavy pan over low fire. **Add** flour and **stir. Continue** cooking until bubbly (about 2 minutes). **Remove** from heat, and **stir in** milk, cream and seasonings. **Return** to heat.

Cook until sauce reaches boiling point, stirring constantly. **Cook** 2 minutes longer or until thick and smooth as cream. **Remove** from heat. **Blend** 4 tablespoons sauce into cannelloni filling.

Cook's Notes:

EGG NOODLES WITH BUTTER AND CHEESE

Fettuccine all'Alfredo

1 recipe Cannelloni dough
   (see p. 86) or 1 lb.
   ready-made Fettuccine
8 qts. water

2 tablespoons salt
1 cup butter
1 cup Parmesan cheese,
   grated

Prepare dough as for Cannelloni recipe. **Divide** dough in half
and roll paper thin with rolling pin or noodle machine. Let
sheets of dough **dry** for 45 minutes. Dough should not be too
dry or sticky. **Roll up** each sheet like jelly roll. **Cut** into ½-inch
slices. **Shake** each to unroll. **Cook** in boiling water (salted) for 4
minutes or until chewy (*al dente*). **Drain,** *but do not rinse.*
Turn noodles into large serving dish. **Add** butter and cheese;
sprinkle with pepper. Using two forks, **toss** about 6 times until
well coated and slightly moist. Serves 6.

Cook's Notes:

GREEN LASAGNE BOLOGNA

Lasagne Verdi alla Bolognese

Dough

2 cups sifted flour
2 eggs, well beaten
¼ cup cooked spinach,
    strained or puréed in

blender, or baby food
1 tablespoon melted butter
or oil

Put flour in large bowl, making a well in the center. **Combine** eggs, spinach and melted butter or oil. **Pour** into well. **Mix** with fork, adding half of flour. **Add** rest of flour and mix with hands. **Knead** until smooth and elastic (about 1 to 2 minutes), adding more flour *if necessary*. (Dough should be medium-soft.) **Roll** dough into ball. **Let stand** 15 minutes at room temperature. **Divide** dough into 4 pieces. **Roll** paper thin on floured board with rolling pin or noodle machine. Allow sheets to **dry** on cloth or floured board 20 to 25 minutes. The dough should not be too dry or sticky. **Roll up** each sheet like jelly roll. **Cut** crosswise into ½-inch slices. **Shake** each to unroll. **Cook** in 8 qts. boiling water salted with 1 tablespoon salt 3 minutes, stirring frequently. **Drain** and **spread** ⅓ of sauce onto bottom of 2 qt. casserole or baking dish. **Cover** with layer of green noodles and sprinkle with cheese. **Repeat** as many times as possible, ending with layer of sauce and cheese. **Bake** at 375° for 25 minutes (if frozen bake uncovered 1¼ hours) or until brown on edges. Serves 6–8.

NOTE: If desired, spread noodles on cloth and dry thoroughly (about 1 to 2 hours). Place in tightly covered container until ready to use. One lb. of ready-made noodles may also be used in this recipe.

Sauce

⅛ lb. salt pork	1½ cups bouillon or water
¼ lb. ground pork	1 tablespoon tomato paste
1 lb. ground veal	¼ teaspoon salt or to taste
¼ lb. ground beef	⅛ teaspoon pepper
1 small carrot, grated	⅛ teaspoon nutmeg
1 onion, minced	½ cup cream
1 stalk celery, minced	

Place salt pork and all ground meats in large saucepan. **Brown** over medium fire, (about 10 minutes) stirring and breaking meats with fork. **Add** carrot, onion and celery to meat mixture. **Sauté** for 2 minutes. **Blend** bouillon with tomato paste and add to meat mixture. **Season** with salt and pepper. **Add** nutmeg. **Simmer** over low fire 1 hour, stirring occasionally. **Add** cream. **Stir** and **cook** 2 minutes longer. Ingredients can be assembled 2 days ahead of time and frozen for as long as six months.

Cook's Notes:

GREEN NOODLES MODENA STYLE

Lasagne alla Modena

1 lb. green homemade
   noodles (see p. 90) or
   ready-made, cooked
   al dente and drained
2 tablespoons butter

½ cup Romano or
   Parmesan cheese, grated
Red Sauce
White Sauce

Butter casserole or large baking dish with 2 tablespoons butter. **Spread** thin layer of red sauce, then white sauce. **Sprinkle** with grated cheese. **Cover** with layer of green noodles. **Repeat** layers until all ingredients are used, ending with layer of red sauce and cheese. **Bake** at 350° for 30 minutes or until bubbly in center. **Let stand** 5 minutes before serving. Can be prepared in advance and refrigerated or frozen. (If refrigerated, bake 1 hour.) Serves 6.

Red Sauce

3 tablespoons oil
2 medium onions, chopped
1 carrot, peeled and grated
4 stalks celery, minced
1 lb. ground beef
⅛ teaspoon nutmeg

½ teaspoon salt
⅛ teaspoon pepper
1 cup dry white wine
1 cup tomatoes, strained or
   put through blender
1 cup heavy cream

Heat oil in saucepan over medium fire. **Add** onions, carrot and celery. **Sauté** 5 minutes, turning occasionally. **Add** ground beef and cook 5 minutes or until it loses red color, breaking meat with fork. **Add** nutmeg, salt, pepper and wine. **Cook** 15 minutes. **Add** tomatoes and continue cooking 45 minutes over low fire. **Remove** from saucepan and cool. **Stir** in cream. **Set aside**

until ready to use. Can be prepared in advance and refrigerated for 2 to 3 days.

White Sauce

½ cup butter
½ cup flour
Pinch white pepper

½ teaspoon salt
1 teaspoon sugar
5 cups milk

Melt butter in saucepan. **Stir** in flour. **Cook** 2 minutes without browning. **Add** remaining ingredients. **Bring** to boil and stir. **Cook** 3 minutes or until thick, stirring constantly to prevent lumps. **Remove** from heat. **Cover** and **set aside** until needed. Can be prepared in advance and refrigerated.

Cook's Notes:

VITO'S STUFFED LASAGNE

Lasagne Imbottite di Vito

Noodle Mixture

1 8-oz. package lasagne noodles	1 cup Romano or Parmesan cheese, grated
4 qts. water	1 lb. ricotta cheese
1 tablespoon oil	1 lb. Provolone or
1 tablespoon salt	mozzarella cheese, sliced

While sauce is cooking, **boil** water in large kettle. **Add** salt and oil. When boiling rapidly, **add** noodles. **Cook** 10 minutes, and **drain.** **Spread** thin layer sauce in bottom of casserole or baking pan. **Sprinkle** with grated cheese. **Place** layer of noodles, then layer of ricotta and sliced cheese. **Spread** sauce and **sprinkle** with grated cheese. **Repeat** layers until all ingredients are used. Top layer should be sauce and grated cheese. **Bake** at 350° for 30 minutes or until sauce is bubbly. **Remove** from oven and **let stand** 10 minutes before **cutting** into squares. Serve with more sauce and sprinkle with grated cheese. Can be prepared in advance and frozen. (If refrigerated, bake 45 minutes or until bubbly.) Serves 6.

Sauce

2 tablespoons olive oil	strained or put through blender
1 clove garlic, minced	
1 small onion, chopped	1 6-oz. can tomato paste
1½ lbs. ground beef	1½ teaspoons salt
2 cups water	⅛ teaspoon pepper
2 16-oz. cans tomatoes,	½ teaspoon basil

Heat oil in saucepan over medium fire. **Add** garlic and onion.

Sauté 3 minutes. **Add** ground meat. **Cook** 5 minutes or until meat loses red color, breaking meat with fork. **Stir in** remaining ingredients. **Reduce** heat to low. **Cook** 1 hour, stirring occasionally. **Set aside** until needed. Can be prepared in advance and refrigerated or frozen.

Cook's Notes:

LITTLE MUFFS

Manicotti

1 recipe basic tomato sauce   1 lb. Manicotti (12
   (see p. 224)   individual Manicotti)
6 qts. water   ¼ cup Parmesan or
1 tablespoon salt   Romano cheese, grated

Prepare sauce. Meantime **boil** 6 qts. water in large kettle with 1 tablespoon salt. **Stir** gently and **cook** over medium fire 5 minutes. **Remove** from heat and put in colander. **Rinse** with 1 cup cold water and shake gently until all water is drained. **Pour** ⅓ of hot sauce into bottom of 8"×8"×2" pan or 2 qt. casserole. **Fill** both ends of Manicotti (a butter knife or a teaspoon will serve this purpose). **Place** Manicotti side by side in rows in baking pan or casserole. **Cover** with sauce; **sprinkle** with cheese. **Bake** in a preheated oven at 375° about 20 minutes or until Manicotti swells and sauce is bubbly. **Lift** Manicotti from pan with pancake turner. Serve hot with more grated cheese. Serves 6.

VARIATION: Use Tufoli instead of Manicotti.

Cheese Filling

1½ lbs. ricotta cheese   1 cup (¼ lb.) mozzarella
½ cup Romano cheese,   cheese, shredded
   grated   ½ teaspoon salt or to taste
2 eggs, well beaten   ⅛ teaspoon pepper or to
                                     taste

Mix all ingredients together and blend well.

Meat Filling

1 tablespoon oil
1 lb. lean ground pork or
   ground beef

1 cup Parmesan or
   Romano cheese, grated
1 cup (½ lb.) ricotta
   cheese
Salt and pepper to taste

Heat oil in skillet over medium fire. **Brown** meat until it loses red color, breaking it up with fork (about 5 minutes). **Drain** off excess fat. **Add** remaining ingredients. **Blend** well.

Chicken Filling

Omit oil and meat from above and **substitute** 2 cups ground cooked chicken. **Proceed** in the same manner.

Vegetable Filling

1½ cups cooked spinach,
   chopped and well drained
2 cups (1 lb.) ricotta
   cheese
1 cup Parmesan cheese,
   grated

Salt and pepper to taste
⅛ teaspoon nutmeg
2 tablespoons bread crumbs

Combine all ingredients and mix well.

Sausage Filling

1 lb. sweet Italian sausage,
   removed from casing
¼ cup Parmesan or
   Romano cheese, grated
1 slice bread, soaked in ¼
   cup water and squeezed

dry, or ½ cup bread
   crumbs
1 egg
¼ teaspoon salt
⅛ teaspoon pepper

Combine all ingredients and mix well.
NOTE: 1 lb. mixed ground pork, veal and beef may be used instead of sausage. **Proceed** in the same manner.

NOODLE AND HAM CASSEROLE

Fettucine con Prosciutto

4 tablespoons butter
4 tablespoons flour
3 cups milk
½ teaspoon salt
⅛ teaspoon pepper
½ lb. green noodles,
cooked until chewy (al
dente) and drained

2 cups prosciutto or cooked
ham, diced
1 cup (¼ lb.) Provolone
or Fontina cheese,
shredded
2 tablespoons Romano
cheese, grated
2 tablespoons parsley,
chopped
Salt if needed

Cook butter and flour in saucepan 2 minutes without browning. **Remove** from heat, and **stir in** milk, salt and pepper. **Return** to heat and **bring to** boil, stirring 1 minute. **Cook** 2 minutes longer, stirring constantly to prevent lumps. **Remove** from heat and **set** aside. **Place** cooked noodles in bowl. **Add** ham, shredded Provolone, grated cheese and parsley. **Toss** well with two forks, and transfer into casserole. **Bake** at 350° for 20 minutes or until bubbly. **Taste** and add more salt if needed. Can be prepared in advance and refrigerated. (If refrigerated, allow 15 minutes more for baking.) Serves 4.

NOTE: Excellent for buffet. Keep warm in chafing dish.

VARIATIONS: *With Tuna*
Substitute 2 7-oz. cans tuna, drained and flaked, omitting 2 cups ham. **Proceed** in same manner.

With Chicken
Substitute 2 cups cooked diced chicken for 2 cups ham. **Proceed** in same manner.

With Mushrooms

Mix with noodles, ham and cheese, 2 3-oz. cans broiled sliced mushrooms, drained.

Serving suggestion: Serve with extra sauce and grated cheese. Accompany with green salad. Serve fruit for dessert. Makes an excellent buffet dish.

Cook's Notes:

NOODLES WITH CHEESE

Lasagne con Formaggio

Noodles

1 recipe Cannelloni Dough
(see p. 86)
6 quarts water
2 tablespoons salt
1 tablespoon oil

1 lb. mozzarella cheese,
thinly sliced
3 tablespoons Romano or
Parmesan cheese, grated

Roll dough paper thin and **cut** into strips 2 inches wide and 10 inches long. In large kettle **bring** water to rapid boil. **Add** salt and oil. (Oil prevents noodles from sticking.) Slowly **drop** noodles into boiling water. **Cook** 5 minutes, stirring occasionally. **Drain** noodles and **spread** on towel or hang on sides of colander until needed. **Spread** one cup sauce into bottom of 13"×9"×2" baking pan, then **spread** a layer of noodles lengthwise. **Spread** ⅓ of ricotta mixture and top with layer of mozzarella slices. **Sprinkle** with ⅓ grated cheese. **Spread** with sauce. **Repeat** layers until all ingredients are used, ending with sauce. Store in refrigerator or freezer until ready to bake.

Bake in preheated oven at 350° for 30 to 45 minutes if ingredients are warm; 45 to 60 minutes if stored in refrigerator; 1¼ to 1½ hours if frozen. **Melt** mozzarella cheese until bubbly. **Remove** from oven and **let stand** at room temperature for 15 minutes. (This prevents spreading.) Remains hot for at least 40 to 45 minutes. When ready to serve, **cut** into squares; **lift** squares with pancake turner. Serves 6–8.

NOTE: This dish is best when made with homemade lasagne, but 1 lb. ready-made lasagne may be substituted. Cook 10 minutes.

Filling

2 eggs, well beaten   ½ cup Romano or
1½ lbs. ricotta cheese   Parmesan cheese, grated

In a bowl combine eggs, ricotta and grated cheese. **Blend** well. **Refrigerate** until ready to use.

Sauce

3 tablespoons olive oil   3 6-oz. cans tomato paste
3 tablespoons onion, minced   6½ cups water
1 clove garlic, minced   1 teaspoon sugar (optional)
1½ lbs. ground beef   1 teaspoon salt
3 links Italian sausage,   ⅛ teaspoon pepper
   removed from casing   6 fresh basil leaves or ½
3½ cups (29-oz. can)   teaspoon dried basil
   Italian plum tomatoes

Heat oil in Dutch oven or large heavy saucepan over medium fire. **Add** onion and garlic. **Cook** 2 to 3 minutes until onion is soft, stirring frequently. **Stir in** ground beef and sausage. **Brown** meat until it loses red color, breaking up with fork (about 5 to 8 minutes). **Strain** tomatoes or put through blender. **Add** tomatoes, tomato paste and water to meat. **Stir** until well blended. **Add** remaining ingredients. Let mixture come to boil. **Reduce** heat to simmer, and **cook** uncovered 2½ hours or until thick, stirring occasionally. **Taste** for seasoning; add salt and pepper if necessary. Sauce may be refrigerated or frozen until ready to use.

NOTE: Sausage may be rolled into marble-size balls and dropped into boiling sauce without browning.

Cook's Notes:

MACARONI AND CHEESE CASSEROLE

Pasticcio di Maccheroni

½ lb. (about 2 cups
  uncooked) elbow
  macaroni, ditali or any
  other short-cut macaroni
1 cup mozzarella or Fontina
  cheese, coarsely grated

1 cup Parmesan cheese,
  grated
4 tablespoons butter
1 cup milk
⅛ teaspoon nutmeg
⅛ teaspoon pepper or to
  taste

Cook macaroni in 4 qts. boiling water salted with 1 tablespoon
salt. **Cook** until tender (about 10 minutes) but still firm. Drain
and place in bowl. **Add** remaining ingredients and toss gently.
Turn into a 2½ qt. casserole greased with 1 teaspoon butter.
Bake at 350° for 30 minutes. Serves 4–5.

Cook's Notes:

Gnocchi

There are endless variations in the preparation of gnocchi (dumplings). Every region in Italy has its own specialty. Gnocchi are made with potatoes, spinach, ricotta, semolina, farina, cream of wheat, cornmeal, butter and egg. Their popularity ranks close to that of the traditional spaghetti. The sauce as well as the gnocchi can be prepared ahead of time. They also may be frozen with splendid results.

Preparing Gnocchi

1. Dry mealy potatoes such as the Idaho are best for making gnocchi. They must be freshly boiled and warm. Do not use leftover mashed potatoes. Very watery potatoes require the addition of more flour.

2. Use potatoes of uniform size so that cooking time will be the same for all. Do not overcook.

3. Since some flours absorb more liquid than others, it is rather difficult to give the exact amount of flour needed. Use your own judgement.

4. To be sure gnocchi mixture contains enough flour, test it by shaping one gnocchi and dropping it into rapidly boiling salted water. If it falls apart add a little more flour.

5. If gnocchi are to be prepared and served immediately, have ready a large kettle containing 8 qts. of water salted with 2 tablespoons of salt. Bring to rapid boil. Drop in gnocchi about 20 at a time. Do not crowd.

6. Do not stir, turn or handle gnocchi roughly during cooking. Gnocchi will rise to surface when thoroughly cooked, which requires only 3 minutes if cooked immediately, or 6 minutes if frozen. Remove cooked gnocchi with strainer or slotted spoon. Drain.

7. To keep cooked gnocchi warm while cooking remaining gnocchi, place in chafing dish or ovenproof dish over a kettle of boiling water. You can also place dish in a skillet half filled with water or an electric skillet filled with water. (Turn to lowest temperature).

8. It is best not to double the gnocchi recipe because the longer the dough stands the softer it gets and the more difficult it becomes to handle. (Potatoes give out moisture.)

Freezing Gnocchi

Gnocchi are readily adaptable to various methods of freezing which can cut a meal's preparation time almost in half. **Rub** 1 teaspoon flour on bottom of cooky sheet, tray, or waxed paper. **Place** gnocchi in single rows about ⅛ inch apart. **Freeze** gnocchi uncovered for about 2½ hours or until frozen solid. **Transfer** to a plastic bag. **Twist** and secure with a rubber band. **Put in** freezer for later use. **Place** gnocchi in layers between double waxed paper or aluminum foil in a heavily waxed paper carton or metal coffee can. **Sprinkle** each layer lightly with flour. **Place** in freezer where they will not be crushed.

To prepare, **fill** a large kettle with 8 qts. water salted with 2 tablespoons salt. **Bring** to rapid boil. **Drop** gnocchi gently into rapidly boiling water a few at a time. *Do not thaw gnocchi* before dropping into boiling water. As soon as they float to the top (about 6 minutes should be allowed to cook unthawed dumplings,) **remove** with strainer or slotted spoon. **Drain. Repeat** until all gnocchi are cooked.

PIEDMONT DUMPLINGS

Gnocchi alla Piemontese

1 lb. (about 3) medium potatoes	¾ cup flour (approx.)
½ teaspoon salt	Tomato sauce (see p. 224)
1 egg yolk, well beaten	3 tablespoons Romano or Parmesan cheese, grated

Scrub potatoes, but do not peel. Place in saucepan and cover with water. Add salt. Cover and cook over medium fire 25 to 40 minutes or until tender when pierced with fork (amount of time depends on size of potatoes). Drain and cover snugly with towel or cloth for 5 minutes, to absorb some of moisture of potatoes; otherwise, they will be mealy. While potatoes are warm, stir in egg. Using your hands, gradually mix in enough flour to make a medium-soft dough (just stiff enough to handle). Turn onto board floured with 2 tablespoons of flour. Knead about 5 times or until ingredients are blended. If dough is sticky, flour hands to knead. Make a test gnocchi and drop in boiling salted water. If it falls apart add more flour. Put a mound of flour on surface. Pinch off piece of dough about the size of an apricot. Roll under palm of hand until about ½ inch thick. Cut into ¾-inch pieces. Toss pieces lightly in mound of flour. Press edge of your thumb into each piece. Pull finger along piece of dough towards you, forming a curl. (Gnocchi may also be shaped by pressing lightly with tines of fork dipped in flour or by pressing gnocchi with thumb against back of a grater.) Arrange gnocchi in single layer on cooky sheet, waxed paper or tray. May be frozen. To serve immediately, drop gnocchi (about 20 at a time) into 8 qts. rapidly boiling, salted water. When gnocchi float (about 3 minutes), remove with perforated spoon to serving dish. Keep warm. When all gnocchi are cooked, cover with sauce and sprinkle with cheese. Serves 4.

FLORENTINE DUMPLINGS

Gnocchi alla Fiorentina

3 medium (about 1½ lbs.)   2 tablespoons melted butter
  potatoes   Butter Sauce or Tomato
1 cup flour   Sauce (see p. 223–224)
¼ cup cream of wheat or   ¼ cup Parmesan or
  farina   Romano cheese, grated
¼ teaspoon salt

Follow directions for Piedmont Dumplings, p. 105. See also "Preparing Gnocchi", pp. 103–104. Can be frozen.

Serving suggestion: Place cooked gnocchi in serving dish. Top with butter or tomato sauce. Sprinkle with grated cheese. Serves 4.

Cook's Notes:

GNOCCHI GENOA STYLE

Gnocchi alla Genovese

2 lbs. (about 6) medium potatoes	½ teaspoon salt
Water to cover	2½ cups flour (approx.)
	Pesto Sauce

Follow directions for Piedmont Dumplings—see p. 105. (See also "Preparing Gnocchi" pp. 103–104.) Serve with the famous Pesto Sauce. This is a fairly soft dough. Do not let it stand too long or dough will become very sticky. (Potatoes give out moisture). If dough does become too soft to handle, sprinkle it with flour and work with floured hands.

Pesto Sauce

2–6 cloves garlic (according to taste), peeled	cheese, grated
1 cup fresh basil leaves	¼ cup pine nuts or walnuts (optional)
1 cup Parmesan or pecorino	1 cup olive oil

Combine in mortar all ingredients except oil. **Pound** with pestle to a paste. **Add** oil gradually and stir with fork until well blended. This is the traditional way of making Pesto in Italy. It can also be blended in an electric blender or placed in a bowl and mashed with a potato masher. The texture will not be as satisfactory as that obtained with the traditional method. Serves 4–6.

NOTE: This sauce can only be made with fresh basil leaves. Basil, "the Queen of the Kitchen," is an easy herb to grow in your garden or in pots. The sauce can be served over various hot pastas (macaroni) and trenetti (fine noodles) about $\frac{1}{16}$ inch wide. A tablespoon of Pesto stirred into Minestrone during the last minute of cooking will enhance the flavor of the soup. Pesto can be frozen or kept in the refrigerator.

GREEN GNOCCHI

Gnocchi Verdi

1 lb. fresh spinach, washed
   and trimmed
2½ lbs. (about 8 medium)
   potatoes
½ teaspoon salt
1 egg, well beaten

2 tablespoons Parmesan
   cheese, grated
½ cup flour (approx.)
Butter and cheese sauce
   (see p. 223)

Place spinach without water in deep saucepan. (Enough water for cooking will cling to leaves.) **Cover** and **cook** over medium fire 5 minutes, stirring occasionally. **Drain** well in colander or sieve. Press out as much liquid as possible with a spoon or saucer. **Let** it cool. **Press** between hands and squeeze until dry. **Grind** or chop finely with knife or scissors. Spinach should look like mush.

Scrub potatoes, but do not peel. **Place** in saucepan and **cover** with water. **Add** salt; **cover** and **cook** over medium fire 25 to 40 minutes or until tender, depending on size of potatoes. **Drain** and **cover** potatoes snugly with towel or cloth for 5 minutes. (This will absorb some of moisture so that potatoes will be mealy). **Peel** and put through ricer or grinder or mash in bowl. There should be no lumps. While potatoes are warm **stir in** spinach, egg and cheese; using hands mix in enough flour to make medium soft dough (just stiff enough to handle). **Turn** onto flat surface floured with 2 tablespoons of flour. **Knead** about 5 times or until ingredients are well blended. To prevent hands from becoming sticky dust with flour. Put mound of flour on surface. **Make** a test gnocchi (one cylinder ½" thick and 2" long). **Roll** in flour. **Drop** into boiling salted water; if it does not hold together add more flour. **Continue** making cylinders;

roll in flour. **Arrange** in single layers on waxed paper, cooky sheet or tray. **Sprinkle** lightly with about 1 tablespoon flour. May be frozen or may be cooked and served immediately. Serves 4–6.

Serving suggestion: Place hot green gnocchi in serving dish. Add butter and cheese sauce. Toss lightly.

Cook's Notes:

MAMA MIA GNOCCHI

Gnocchi di Mama Mia

6 medium (about 2 lbs.)
  potatoes
½ cup semolina (preferred),
  cream of wheat or farina
1 cup flour

2 eggs, well beaten
Mama Mia Ragout Sauce
  (see p. 227)
¼ cup Romano or
  Parmesan cheese, grated

Follow directions for Piedmont Dumplings—see p. 105. Serves 4–6.

NOTE: Semolina can be purchased at any Italian store. Semolina has a fairly high protein content and is very nutritious.

Serving suggestion: Place dumplings on hot platter. Pour sauce over and sprinkle with cheese. Arrange meat around dumplings. Serve hot.

Cook's Notes:

GNOCCHI WITH NUTMEG

Gnocchi con Noce Moscata

6 medium (about 2 lbs.) potatoes
¼ cup farina or cream of wheat

¾ cup flour
2 eggs, well beaten
½ teaspoon nutmeg

Follow directions for Piedmont Dumplings—see p. 105. (See also "Preparing Gnocchi"—pp. 103–104.) Serve with Tomato Sauce, Butter Sauce or Pesto Sauce. See p. 224, p. 223, and p. 107, respectively. Serves 4–6.

Serving suggestion: Place gnocchi in serving dish. Pour sauce. Toss lightly. Serve hot.

Cook's Notes:

PHILOMENA'S DUMPLINGS

Gnocchi di Filomena

1 large (about ¾ lb.)
    potato, peeled
Water to cover (about 1¾
    cups)
½ teaspoon salt

1 egg, beaten
3 cups flour, more if
    necessary
Roll-ups
Sauce

Follow recipe for Piedmont Dumplings (p. 105). **Place** cooked gnocchi on large platter. **Serve** hot with Philomena's Roll-ups, sauce, and sprinkle generously with grated Parmesan cheese.

Roll-ups

2 lbs. top or bottom round
    of beef, sliced ¼ inch
    thick (or thinner) and
    cut into 4 pieces
1 tablespoon oil
2 tablespoons parsley,
    chopped
½ cup bread crumbs
2 tablespoons Romano
    cheese, grated

1 clove garlic, chopped
3 thin slices prosciutto,
    salami, or ham cut into
    small pieces
¼ teaspoon salt
⅛ teaspoon pepper
1 tablespoon tomato juice
2 hard-boiled eggs, sliced
¼ cup olive oil

Brush insides of pieces of meat with 1 tablespoon oil. **Combine** parsley, bread crumbs, cheese, garlic, prosciutto, salt, pepper and tomato juice in bowl. **Mix** thoroughly. **Divide** filling into 4 parts and spread on each side of pieces of meat. **Distribute** egg slices over meat. **Roll up** each slice as tightly as possible like jelly roll. **Tie** securely with cotton string. **Heat** ¼ cup oil in large skillet. **Brown** meat rolls on all sides over medium heat (about 10 minutes), turning occasionally. **Remove** and set aside. Meanwhile, **prepare** sauce.

Sauce

1 small onion, chopped	6 cups water
1 clove garlic, minced	Salt and pepper to taste
2 6-oz. cans tomato paste	

In same skillet, **sauté** onion and garlic for 2 minutes; **stir; add** additional oil if necessary. **Stir** in tomato paste and water until blended. **Season** with salt and pepper. **Transfer** sauce to Dutch oven or deep saucepan. **Bring** to boil and **add** meat rolls. **Lower** heat and **simmer** uncovered about 2 hours or until meat is tender. **Remove** rolls from sauce and **let stand** for 5 minutes for easier slicing. **Remove** string and **cut** rolls into 2-inch slices with sharp knife. Sauce can be prepared in advance and refrigerated or frozen until ready to use.

NOTE: This sauce is good for ravioli, lasagne, pasta and rice. It may be served over 1 lb. cooked spaghetti or macaroni. The sauce recipe was contributed by my sister Philomena, an excellent cook.

VARIATION: *With Spareribs*
Brown 1 lb. spareribs, cut into serving pieces, for 8 to 10 minutes in same skillet used for browning roll-ups. **Turn** often. **Add** to sauce with roll-ups.

Cook's Notes:

RICOTTA DUMPLINGS

Gnocchi di Ricotta

1 lb. ricotta (drained in
colander if watery)
2 tablespoons melted butter
1 egg yolk, well beaten
½ teaspoon salt
2 cups flour

Tomato sauce (see p. 224)
Romano or Parmesan
cheese, grated (amount
depends on number of
layers being made)

Combine ricotta, butter, egg yolk and salt. **Beat** until blended.
Add flour and mix with hands. **Turn** onto floured surface and
knead about 5 times or until ingredients are blended. (If dough
is sticky flour your hands.) **Put** a small mound of flour on surface.
Make a test gnocchi; drop it in boiling water. If it falls apart
add more flour. **Pinch** off pieces of dough about the size of an
apricot. **Roll** into ropelike strips about ¾ inch thick. **Cut** strips
into small pieces about the size of an olive (1 inch). **Toss** pieces
in mound of flour. **Press** edge of your thumb into each piece.
Pull finger along piece of dough towards you, or press lightly
with tines of fork or press gnocchi with thumb against grater.
Serve immediately or freeze for later use. To serve immediately,
heat 8 qts. water salted with 2 tablespoons of salt. **Bring** to a
rolling boil. **Drop** ⅓ of gnocchi into water. **Cook** until they
float to the top (about 3 minutes); remove with strainer or
slotted spoon. **Drain** and **place** in serving dish. When one layer
is completed, **cover** with ⅓ of Tomato Sauce and **sprinkle** with
1 tablespoon grated Romano or Parmesan cheese. **Repeat** until
all gnocchi are cooked. Keep warm. (See also "Preparing Gnocchi"—pp. 103–104.) Serves 4.

NOTE: This dough may also be used to make noodles, which can
be frozen after they dry at room temperature. Freeze in lined waxed
box.

VARIATIONS: *Gnocchi Parmigiana*
Follow above recipe adding 1 cup grated Parmesan cheese with flour.

Ricotta #2
Omit egg yolk and butter from above recipe. **Increase** flour to 4 cups. **Combine** with ricotta and salt. Proceed in the same manner. These gnocchi will be firmer in texture. Cook all at one time in 8 qts. boiling salted water. **Drain** in colander. **Put** into serving dish or bowl, and **pour** any desired tomato sauce over gnocchi and sprinkle with grated Parmesan or Romano cheese. Serve hot.

Cook's Notes:

SEMOLINA DUMPLINGS
Gnocchi di Semolina

1 qt. milk	½ cup butter
½ teaspoon salt	1 cup Parmesan cheese,
1 cup semolina (cream of	grated
wheat)	4 eggs

In heavy saucepan or Dutch oven **bring** milk and salt to a boil. **Lower** heat and gradually **add** semolina, stirring constantly to prevent sticking. **Continue** cooking, stirring until mixture is thickened (about 10 minutes). **Remove** from stove and **stir in** 2 tablespoons butter and ½ cup grated cheese. **Beat in** eggs one at a time until smooth. **Rinse** cooky sheet with cold water or grease with butter, to prevent sticking. **Spread** evenly with ½ inch layer of cooked mixture. **Cool** until firm (about 2 hours), or refrigerate. **Cut** into 1 inch strips or squares with a thin bladed knife. Occasionally dip knife in cold water to prevent sticking. **Place** layer of gnocchi on bottom of 3 qt. buttered casserole or baking dish. **Dot** with remaining butter and cheese. **Repeat** procedure; don't sprinkle top layer with cheese. **Bake** at 375° for 15 minutes or until lightly brown. May be prepared well in advance. Do not freeze longer than 1 month.

VARIATION: Omit remaining butter and cheese and spread layers with any favorite sauce, such as tomato sauce or Bologna Meat Sauce.

Cook's Notes:

LENTILS AND MACARONI

Lenticche e Pasta

1 cup (½ lb.) dried
  lentils
2½ qts. cold water
3 tablespoons olive oil or
  salad oil
1 medium onion, finely
  chopped
1 clove garlic, minced
2 ripe fresh tomatoes, peeled
  and chopped, or 1 cup

canned tomatoes
1 tablespoon parsley,
  chopped
Salt and pepper to taste
½ lb. ditalini macaroni or
  elbow macaroni, cooked
  and drained
¼ cup Parmesan cheese,
  grated

Place lentils in Dutch oven or large saucepan. **Add** water and simmer over low fire 30 minutes or until tender but not mushy. Meanwhile **heat** oil in small skillet. **Sauté** onion and garlic for 2 minutes. **Stir** and **add** tomatoes, parsley, and seasonings. **Simmer** 5 minutes longer, stirring occasionally. **Stir** this mixture into lentils and cook 10 minutes longer. **Add** macaroni and **cook** about 3 minutes longer, stirring frequently. **Serve** in large casserole or serving bowl. **Sprinkle** with cheese. Preparing this dish in advance improves the flavor. May also be frozen. Do not overcook. Serves 4–6.

Cook's Notes:

SPINACH AND CHEESE BALLS
Gnocchi di Spinaci e Formaggio

1 lb. fresh spinach or 2
10-oz. boxes frozen
chopped spinach
1 lb. (2 cups) ricotta
cheese, drained in
colander or sieve
½ teaspoon salt
2 egg yolks
½ cup flour

¼ teaspoon nutmeg
(optional)
2 tablespoons Parmesan
cheese, grated
Choice of sauce—Butter
(p. 223) or Bologna Meat
(p. 232)
Grated cheese

Wash fresh spinach thoroughly and remove coarse stems.
Place in large saucepan without water. (Enough water for
cooking will cling on leaves.) **Sprinkle** with salt. **Cover** and
cook over low fire 5 minutes, stirring occasionally to prevent
sticking. **Drain** well in colander or sieve. **Press** out as much
liquid as possible with back of large spoon. Let it cool. **Press**
between hands and squeeze until quite dry. **Put** through
food grinder using a fine blade, or chop finely with scissors
or knife until it looks like mush. **Add** drained ricotta
and remaining ingredients. **Stir** until well blended. Dough
should be soft, the consistency of drop-cookie dough. **Flour**
hands. **Put** a mound of flour on board or table top. **Roll**
1 teaspoon of mixture into flour and shape with hands into a
ball. **Test** in boiling salted water. If it does not hold together
while cooking add about 1 tablespoon more flour to dough.
Put finished balls on floured cooky sheet or tray, about ⅛
inch apart. Can be frozen. (See "Freezing Gnocchi"—p.
104.) To serve, **heat** 3 qts. water salted with 1 tablespoon
of salt. **Bring** to a boil and **drop** gently into kettle with pancake turner or spatula. **Cook** a few balls at a time until they
float to the top (about 3 minutes). Lift out with strainer

or slotted spoon. Place in casserole or serving dish and keep
warm over hot water while cooking remaining gnocchi. Pour
hot sauce over and sprinkle with grated cheese. Serve hot.
Serves 4.

Cook's Notes:

STUFFED SHELLS

Conchiglia Imbottita

Shells

6 qts. water	1 lb. jumbo stuffing shells
1 tablespoon salt	2 tablespoons Romano
1 tablespoon oil	cheese, grated

Boil water in large kettle. **Add** salt, oil and jumbo shells. **Boil** gently for 10 minutes. **Drain,** and **stuff** each shell with filling. **Close** to prevent filling from falling out. **Arrange** filled shells side by side in oblong casserole or deep baking pan. **Pour** ¾ sauce over all. **Sprinkle** with grated cheese. **Bake** in preheated oven at 375° for 35 minutes or until bubbly. **Serve** with remaining sauce. Can be prepared in advance and stored in refrigerator or frozen. Increase baking time 15 to 20 minutes if prepared in advance. Serves 4–6.

Filling

1½ lbs. ricotta or creamy cottage cheese	2 tablespoons parsley chopped
½ cup Romano cheese, grated	2 eggs, slightly beaten
1 cup Provolone or Mozzarella, shredded	½ teaspoon salt
	⅛ teaspoon pepper

Combine all ingredients in bowl, and **mix** thoroughly. **Refrigerate** until ready to use.

Sauce

2 tablespoons olive oil	2½ cups water
1 small onion, minced	1 teaspoon salt
1 lb. ground beef	¼ teaspoon freshly ground
2 6-oz. cans tomato paste	pepper
1 1 lb., 12-oz. can tomato	4 fresh basil leaves or ¼
purée	teaspoon basil

Heat oil in saucepan over medium fire. **Stir in** onion, and **sauté** 2 minutes, stirring constantly. **Add** ground meat and **cook** until it loses red color (about 5 minutes), breaking meat with fork as it cooks. **Stir in** remaining ingredients. **Bring to** boil. **Reduce** to low fire. **Simmer** uncovered 1 hour or until thick, stirring often. **Taste** and add more seasoning if necessary.

Cook's Notes:

RAVIOLI

Dough

1½ teaspoons oil or melted   1 egg, beaten
   butter   2 cups flour (approx.)
½ cup lukewarm water

Combine oil or melted butter, water and egg in bowl. With fingers **work in** enough flour to form medium dough. **Knead** for 1 minute or until smooth; form into a ball. Add more flour if dough is too sticky or more water if dough is too dry. **Cover** with bowl and **let rest** for 30 minutes. **Divide** dough into two parts, and **roll out** each half on lightly floured board until paper thin. **Place** 1 teaspoon filling in mounds about 2 inches apart on one sheet of dough. **Cover** with the other sheet. **Press** with fingers around each mound. **Cut** into squares with knife or pastry cutter. **Press** cut edges with tines of fork so that filling will not fall out. **Place** on lightly floured wax paper or towel. **Let dry** for 1 hour, turning after first ½ hour.

To cook, **drop** gently into large kettle of rapidly boiling salted water (2 tablespoons salt to 8 qts. water). **Cook** 8 to 10 minutes or until tender, depending on thickness. **Remove** with strainer or slotted spoon to platter or individual plates. To serve, cover with sauce and sprinkle with 3 tablespoons grated Romano or Parmesan cheese. Serve hot. Serves 4–6.

NOTE: Filled ravioli can be prepared in advance. Place between layers of waxed paper on cooky sheet and refrigerate or freeze until ready to cook.

Ricotta Filling

1 lb. fresh ricotta cheese
1 egg
1 cup Romano or Parmesan cheese, grated

¼ cup parsley, chopped
½ teaspoon salt or to taste
⅛ teaspoon pepper

Place all ingredients in bowl and **mix** thoroughly until smooth. Refrigerate until ready to use.

Chicken Filling

2 cups cooked chicken, ground
½ clove garlic, minced
¼ cup parsley, chopped
½ cup Romano or Parmesan cheese, grated

½ cup bread crumbs
1 teaspoon salt or to taste
⅛ teaspoon pepper
½ cup cooked spinach, drained
2 eggs, beaten
⅛ teaspoon nutmeg

Combine all ingredients in bowl and **mix** thoroughly.

Meat Filling

1 tablespoon oil
1 lb. ground lean pork or mixture of pork and veal
½ cup Fontina or Parmesan cheese, grated
2 eggs, beaten

1 lb. ricotta cheese
1 teaspoon salt or to taste
⅛ teaspoon pepper
2 tablespoons parsley, chopped

Heat oil in skillet over medium flame. **Cook** meat until it loses red color (about 5 to 8 minutes), breaking up with fork. **Remove** from heat and **drain off** excess fat. **Stir in** grated cheese. **Add** remaining ingredients and **mix** thoroughly.

Sausage Filling

1 tablespoon oil	½ cup bread crumbs
1 lb. mild Italian sausage, casing removed	1 lb. ricotta cheese
	2 eggs, beaten
½ cup Fontina or Parmesan cheese, grated	¼ cup parsley, chopped
	Salt and pepper to taste

Follow directions for meat filling.

NOTE: Ravioli fillings can be prepared in advance and refrigerated or frozen until needed.

Tomato Sauce

2 tablespoons olive oil	9 tomato paste cans of water
1 clove garlic	
1 small onion, chopped	½ teaspoon basil
3 6-oz. cans tomato paste	Salt and pepper to taste

Heat oil in deep saucepan. Add garlic and onions. **Sauté** over medium heat 2 minutes or until brown. **Stir in** remaining ingredients, blending well. Bring to **boil** and reduce heat. **Simmer** 2½ hours over low heat or until sauce reaches consistency of thick cream; stir occasionally.

NOTE: Sauce may be prepared in advance and frozen.

Cook's Notes:

MACARONI WITH RICOTTA

Pasta con Ricotta

1 lb. ricotta cheese
½ cup Parmesan or
   Fontina cheese, grated
½ cup water or milk
2 tablespoons olive oil

1 teaspoon salt or to taste
⅛ teaspoon pepper
1 lb. ditali or any short
   macaroni

Combine in bowl ricotta cheese, grated cheese, water, olive oil, salt and pepper. **Beat** until smooth and set aside. **Cook** macaroni according to instructions on package until chewy (al dente). **Drain** and **place** in casserole or serving dish. **Pour** ricotta mixture over and toss with two forks to coat. Keep warm over warmer or in oven. Serves 4–6.

Cook's Notes:

SPAGHETTI WITH MEATBALLS

Pasta con Sugo e Polpette

Sauce

2 tablespoons olive oil
2 tablespoons onion, minced
  or 1 clove garlic, minced
3 6-oz. cans tomato paste

12 tomato paste cans water
¼ teaspoon basil (optional)
1 teaspoon sugar (optional)
Salt and pepper to taste

Heat oil in saucepan. Add onion or garlic and sauté 2 minutes over medium heat. Stir in remaining ingredients and blend well. Bring to boil. Lower heat and cook 2½ hours, stirring occasionally.

Meatballs

2 slices bread
1 lb. ground beef, or ¾ lb.
  beef and ¼ lb. pork, or
  combination of beef, pork
  and veal
1 egg

1 tablespoon parsley,
  chopped
1 clove garlic, minced or 1
  tablespoon onion, chopped
1 teaspoon salt
⅛ teaspoon pepper or to
  taste
2 tablespoons oil

Soak bread in ½ cup cold water for 5 minutes. Squeeze dry. Combine all ingredients except oil in bowl. Mix thoroughly with hands, and shape into balls about 1½ inches in diameter (size of a small egg). Heat 2 tablespoons oil in skillet. Brown meatballs quickly on all sides (about 5 to 6 minutes), but do not cook all the way through. Add meatballs to sauce after it has been cooking ½ hour. Simmer in sauce 2 hours. Sauce and meatballs may be prepared in advance and refrigerated for 1 week or frozen.

Spaghetti

Bring 5 qts. salted water (1 tablespoon salt) to a rolling **boil**. **Add** 1 lb. spaghetti and **cook** 12 minutes or until tender but chewy (*al dente*). Stir occasionally. **Remove** from heat and **add** 1 cup cold water. **Drain** and turn into a serving dish or casserole. **Add** part of sauce. **Sprinkle** with grated Parmesan cheese. With two forks, lift spaghetti up and down to coat with sauce. Pass additional sauce, cheese, and meatballs when serving. Serves 6.

NOTE: Any type of macaroni may be substituted for spaghetti.

VARIATIONS: *With Sparerib Sauce*
Substitute spareribs (cut into 2-rib portions) for meatballs. **Brown** on both sides about 6 to 8 minutes. **Add** to sauce after it is blended. Proceed as in meatball recipe.

With Italian Sweet Sausage
Substitute sausage for meatballs. **Brown** sausage on all sides (about 5 minutes). When sausage is browned, **add** it to the blended sauce. Proceed as in meatball recipe.

Cook's Notes:

Vegetables

ASPARAGUS CASSEROLE

Casseruola di Asparagi

2 lbs. fresh asparagus
2 qts. boiling salted water
1 cup reserved asparagus
  liquid
2 tablespoons butter
2 tablespoons shallots or
  scallions, minced
2 tablespoons flour

¼ cup Fontina cheese,
  shredded
⅛ teaspoon pepper
¼ cup Parmesan cheese,
  grated
¼ teaspoon rosemary,
  crushed
¼ cup bread crumbs
¼ cup Provolone cheese,
  shredded

Wash asparagus and cut off tough end stalks. Cook in boiling salted water 10 minutes. Drain and reserve 1 cup asparagus liquid. Melt butter in skillet over medium heat. Stir in minced shallots or scallions and cook 1 minute. Blend in flour and cook 2 minutes without browning. Add reserved asparagus liquid. Bring to boil, stirring constantly. Stir in Fontina cheese, pepper, Parmesan cheese and rosemary. Cook 1 minute longer or until cheese is melted. Pour over asparagus in casserole. Sprinkle with bread crumbs and Provolone. Bake at 375° for 15 to 20 minutes or until bubbly. Can be prepared in advance and refrigerated. (If refrigerated, bake 30 minutes.) Serves 4.

NOTE: Excellent buffet dish. Can be prepared in chafing dish.

VARIATION: Substitute 2 lbs. fresh broccoli or brussels sprouts for asparagus. If using brussels sprouts, cook only 5 minutes. Proceed as for asparagus.

Cook's Notes:

ASPARAGUS WITH CHEESE

Asparagi con Formaggio

2 lbs. fresh asparagus	½ cup Parmesan cheese,
2 quarts boiling salted water	grated
½ cup melted butter	

Wash asparagus and **cut off** tough end stalks. **Cook** in boiling salted water for 10 minutes. **Drain** and **arrange** a layer of asparagus in casserole. **Drizzle** butter over them and **sprinkle** with cheese. **Repeat** layers. **Bake** at 400° for 5 to 10 minutes or until tender. Serves 4.

VARIATION: *With Broccoli*
Substitute 2 lbs. fresh broccoli for asparagus. Proceed in same manner.

Cook's Notes:

ASPARAGUS WITH MACARONI

Pasta con Asparagi

2 lbs. fresh asparagus
¼ cup olive oil
2 cloves garlic
1 1 lb., 12-oz. can plum
   tomatoes

2 tablespoons parsley,
   chopped
Salt and pepper to taste
1 lb. spiedini (spiral short
   macaroni)

Wash asparagus, cut off tough end stalks and cut in half. **Heat** oil in saucepan over low fire. **Add** garlic and asparagus. **Sauté** 10 minutes, turning occasionally. **Add** tomatoes, parsley, salt and pepper. **Cover** and **cook** 45 minutes, turning occasionally to prevent sticking. **Cook** macaroni according to instructions on package until chewy (al dente). **Drain** and **place** in heated serving dish or casserole. **Pour** on asparagus sauce and **sprinkle** with cheese. **Toss** with two forks. Asparagus sauce can be prepared in advance and refrigerated or frozen. Serves 4–6.

Cook's Notes:

CABBAGE ROLLS

Cavoli Ripieni

10 large cabbage leaves
1 cup cooked rice
1½ lbs. ground beef or
   pork, or mixture of both
1 medium onion, minced
1½ teaspoons salt
⅛ teaspoon pepper
2 tablespoons parsley,
   minced

¼ teaspoon sage
½ cup Provolone cheese,
   shredded
½ cup Fontina cheese,
   grated
1 29-oz. can (3½ cups)
   tomatoes

Drop cabbage leaves into boiling water and **simmer** until limp but not soft (about 3 minutes). **Drain** and **cool.** Meanwhile **combine** rice, ground meat, onion, salt, pepper, parsley, sage, Provolone and Fontina in large bowl. **Mix** with hands to blend together. **Divide** meat mixture into 10 parts. **Shape** each part into roll. **Place** meat roll in center of each leaf. **Roll** each leaf around meat and fold ends under. **Secure** with toothpick and lay in single layer in casserole, folded side down. **Crush** tomatoes with fingers or purée in blender. **Spread** over cabbage rolls. **Bake** at 350° for 1½ hours or until tender. Check occasionally. Can be prepared in advance and stored in refrigerator or frozen. Serves 5.

Cook's Notes:

SAVORY CABBAGE

Cavolo

10 large savory cabbage
  leaves
1 lb. ground beef
¼ cup onion, minced
¾ cup bread crumbs
2 tablespoons water
2 tablespoons parsley,
  chopped
1 egg

1 teaspoon salt
⅛ teaspoon pepper
¼ teaspoon allspice
¼ cup Romano or Fontina
  cheese, grated
¼ cup melted butter
1 cup bouillon or water

Drop cabbage leaves into boiling water and **simmer** until limp but not soft (about 3 minutes). **Drain** and **cool.** Meanwhile **combine** meat, onion, bread crumbs, water, parsley, egg, salt, pepper, allspice and cheese in large bowl. **Mix** with hands to blend together. **Divide** meat mixture into 10 parts. **Shape** into balls and **place** meatball in center of each cabbage leaf. **Fold** top leaf over and **secure** with toothpick. **Lay** in single layer in oval casserole or baking dish. **Pour** butter and bouillon over cabbage. **Bake** at 350° for 1½ hours or until tender. Check occasionally adding bouillon or water if necessary. Can be prepared in advance and stored in refrigerator or frozen. Serves 5.

Cook's Notes:

CABBAGE CASSEROLE

Casseruola di Cavolo

1 medium head cabbage
4 tablespoons butter or
   margarine
1 medium onion, chopped
2 cups warm water,
   chicken bouillon or
   tomato juice
4 medium potatoes, peeled
   and thinly sliced

½ cup raw rice
¼ teaspoon dry basil or
   sage (optional)
Salt and pepper to taste
½ cup Parmesan or
   Romano cheese, grated

Wash cabbage and shred. **Set** aside. **Melt** butter or margarine
in saucepan. **Add** onion and **sauté** over low fire. **Stir** and **add**
cabbage. **Sauté** 5 minutes longer. **Remove** from heat and **add**
water, bouillon or tomato juice. **Stir** to blend well. **Transfer** to
2½ qt. casserole or small roasting pan. **Top** with potatoes and
sprinkle with rice, sage, salt, pepper and cheese. **Cover** and bake
at 350° for 25 minutes. **Remove** cover and bake 10 minutes
longer or until potatoes and rice are tender. Add boiling hot
water if too dry. Serves 4–5.

VARIATION: **Add** browned pork chops on top of layer of potatoes.

Cook's Notes:

CORNMEAL CASSEROLE

Casseruola di Polenta

1 cup cornmeal
3 tablespoons butter
1 lb. fresh mushrooms,
   sliced
1 cup tomato sauce or 1
   8-oz. can tomatoes

½ cup Parmesan cheese,
   grated
Freshly ground pepper to
   taste

Cook cornmeal according to label on package. **Turn** cooked cornmeal into greased 2 qt. casserole. **Level** top of cornmeal with spoon. **Melt** butter in skillet and **sauté** mushrooms 3 minutes. **Add** tomato sauce and **stir. Pour** over cooked cornmeal. **Sprinkle** with cheese and pepper. **Bake** in preheated oven at 350° for 30 minutes. Serves 4–6.

Cook's Notes:

CAULIFLOWER

Cavolfiore

1 medium head cauliflower	1½ cups milk
1 cup water	1 cup Fontina cheese,
¼ teaspoon salt	shredded
2 tablespoons butter or	2 cups cooked ham, diced
margarine	½ cup bread crumbs
2 tablespoons flour	1 tablespoon melted butter

Remove outer leaves, core and stalk of cauliflower. Wash and cut into thin slices. Cook in boiling, salted water for 5 minutes or until tender but not mushy. Drain and arrange in bottom of casserole. Cook butter and flour in skillet 2 minutes without browning. Stir in milk and bring to boil, stirring 1 minute. Cook 2 minutes longer, stirring constantly. Stir in cheese. Remove from heat. Sprinkle ham over cauliflower. Pour cheese sauce over. Mix together bread crumbs and melted butter. Sprinkle over top. Bake at 350° for 35 minutes or until crumbs are browned. Can be prepared in advance and refrigerated. (If refrigerated, bake for 50 minutes.) Serves 6.

Cook's Notes:

CAULIFLOWER MILANESE STYLE

Cavolfiore alla Milanese

1 large cauliflower
1 cup water
½ teaspoon salt
4 tablespoons olive oil
4 medium onions, sliced
10 ripe olives, pitted and
    chopped

1 cup (¼ lb.) Provolone
    cheese, shredded
2 tablespoons Parmesan
    cheese, grated
⅛ teaspoon pepper
1 cup white wine

Remove outer leaves, core and stalk of cauliflower. Wash and cut into thin slices. Add cauliflower to salted boiling water. Cook 5 minutes or until tender but not mushy. Drain. Grease casserole with olive oil. Place a thin layer of onions on bottom. Add a layer of olives and a layer of cauliflower. Sprinkle with Provolone, Parmesan cheese, and pepper. Repeat layers until all ingredients are used up. Then pour wine over. Bake at 350° for 35 minutes. Can be prepared in advance and refrigerated. (If refrigerated, allow 15 minutes more for baking.) Serves 4.

Cook's Notes:

GREEN BEANS

Fagiolini

4 tablespoons olive oil
2 medium onions, sliced
1 clove garlic, minced
1 1 lb., 12-oz. can (3½
    cups) tomatoes, mashed
1½ teaspoons salt

¼ teaspoon freshly ground
    pepper
¼ teaspoon basil or oregano
1½ lbs. green beans, whole
    or cut
3 medium potatoes, peeled
    and quartered

Heat oil over medium heat in casserole. **Sauté** onions and garlic for 2 minutes. **Add** tomatoes, salt, pepper and basil or oregano. **Bring** to boil. **Add** beans and potatoes. **Cover** and **cook** 30 minutes or until vegetables are tender, stirring occasionally to prevent sticking. Can be prepared in advance and stored in refrigerator or frozen. (If freezing, omit potatoes.) Serves 4.

Cook's Notes:

PEAS WITH LINGUINE

Pasta e Piselli

3 tablespoons butter or olive oil
1 medium onion, chopped
3 slices bacon or prosciutto, diced
1 cup water
1 lb. peas, shelled or 1 10-oz. package frozen peas

2 tablespoons parsley, chopped
1 teaspoon salt
⅛ teaspoon pepper
1 lb. linguine (narrow noodles)
½ cup Parmesan cheese, grated

In large skillet, **cook** onion in butter or olive oil for 5 minutes or until soft. **Add** bacon and cook 2 minutes longer. **Add** water, peas, parsley, salt and pepper. **Cook** 20 minutes or until peas are soft, stirring occasionally. While peas are cooking, **cook** noodles according to instructions on package until chewy (*al dente*). **Drain** and **place** in casserole or serving dish. **Sprinkle** with cheese, **pour** hot pea sauce over noodles and toss. **Keep warm** in oven until ready to serve. Pea sauce can be prepared in advance and refrigerated or frozen. Serves 4–6.

Cook's Notes:

SICILIAN PEPPERS

Peperoni alla Siciliana

4 large green peppers
1 cup bread crumbs
6 anchovy filets, chopped
2 tablespoons raisins
2 tablespoons pine nuts
¼ teaspoon salt
⅛ teaspoon pepper
½ cup olive oil

1 fresh tomato, peeled and
   chopped
¼ teaspoon basil
2 tablespoons parsley,
   chopped
10 ripe olives, pitted and
   chopped
4 teaspoons olive oil
½ cup tomato sauce

Cut thin slice from top of each pepper. **Remove** seeds and pulp. **Combine** in bowl all ingredients except the 4 teaspoons olive oil and the tomato sauce. **Mix** thoroughly with hands. **Stuff** peppers with mixture. **Stand** stuffed peppers upright in casserole. **Drizzle** oil over peppers and top each with 1 tablespoon tomato sauce. **Pour** remaining sauce around peppers. **Cover.** **Bake** in preheated oven at 375° for 45 minutes or until peppers are done. Check occasionally. Can be prepared in advance and stored in refrigerator or frozen. Serves 4.

Cook's Notes:

PEPPERS WITH RICE

Peperoni con Risotto

4 large green peppers
2 tablespoons butter
2 links Italian sausage, removed from casing
1 small onion, chopped
1 cup rice

3 cubes bouillon
2 tablespoons Romano cheese, grated
Salt and pepper to taste
2 tablespoons olive oil
2 tablespoons tomato paste

Cut thin slice from top of each pepper. Remove seeds and pulp. Set aside. Melt butter over medium heat in skillet. Sauté sausage and onion 5 minutes, breaking sausage with fork. Add rice, and stir constantly 5 minutes. Add bouillon, dissolved in 3 cups hot water and reduce heat to low. Cover and cook 14 minutes. Remove from heat and stir in cheese. Taste for seasoning and let cool. Stuff peppers with mixture. Grease casserole with oil. Stand stuffed peppers upright. Pour tomato paste (mixed with 1 cup hot water) around peppers. Bake at 350° for 30 minutes or until peppers are done. Check occasionally. Can be prepared in advance and stored in refrigerator or frozen. Serves 4.

Cook's Notes:

PEPPERS WITH HOMEMADE SAUSAGE

Peperoni con Salsiccia

3 tablespoons oil
Homemade sausage (see
  recipe below)
4 green peppers, cut into
  1-inch strips

4 medium potatoes, peeled
  and thinly sliced
1 onion, thinly sliced
½ teaspoon salt
⅛ teaspoon pepper
¼ cup water

Heat oil in skillet over medium fire. Fry sausage on all sides
for 20 minutes, pricking in several places with fork.

Remove and place in casserole. In same skillet, place peppers,
potatoes and onions. Season with salt and pepper. Cover and
cook 15 minutes, turning occasionally to prevent sticking. Pour
vegetable mixture over sausage. Add water, cover and continue
cooking 15 minutes or until tender. Serves 4–6.

Sausage Mixture

1 teaspoon fennel seeds
2 lbs. coarsely ground pork
  shoulder or butt
½ teaspoon pepper or to
  taste
2 teaspoons salt
¼ cup Provolone, Fontina

or Caciovallo cheese,
  shredded
1 tablespoon parsley,
  chopped
Sausage casings, soaked in
  cold water and drained

Combine fennel seeds, meat, pepper, salt, cheese and parsley in bowl. Mix thoroughly with hands. Stuff meat mixture into
casings with sausage funnel. Tie every four inches or twist in
center. Store in refrigerator until ready to use.

NOTE: For hot sausage, add 1 teaspoon hot red pepper seeds
to sausage mixture.

Serving suggestion: Serve broiled or grilled sausage with sautéed green peppers in Italian roll or long loaf bread cut into 3-inch slices. Makes excellent luncheon, supper or party meal.

Cook's Notes:

CHEESE-STUFFED PEPPERS

Peperoni Ripieni con Formaggio

4 large green peppers
1 lb. ground beef
4 slices bread, soaked in
    water for 5 minutes and
    squeezed dry
1 medium onion, chopped
¼ cup Fontina or
    Parmesan cheese, grated

1 egg
1 teaspoon salt
⅛ teaspoon pepper
2 tablespoons parsley,
    chopped
2 cups or 2 8-oz. cans
    tomato sauce
4 thin slices Provolone
    cheese

Cut thin slice from top of each pepper. **Remove** seeds and pulp. **Combine** beef, bread, onion, grated cheese, egg, salt, pepper and parsley in bowl. **Mix** well with hands and **stuff** peppers with mixture. **Stand** stuffed peppers upright in casserole. **Pour** sauce around peppers. **Top** each pepper with slice of Provolone. **Bake** uncovered in preheated oven at 350° for 1 hour or until peppers are done. Check occasionally. Can be prepared in advance and stored in refrigerator or frozen. Serves 4.

Cook's Notes:

EGGS WITH PEPPERS

Uova con Peperoni

3 large firm green peppers
¼ cup olive oil
2 onions, thinly sliced
  (optional)

6 eggs
Salt and pepper to taste

Wash peppers. Remove seeds, stem and pith. Slice lengthwise into 1-inch strips. Heat oil in chafing dish or electric frying pan. Add cleaned peppers and sliced onion. Sauté 15 to 18 minutes or until peppers are soft. Beat eggs. Add salt and pepper. Fold in beaten eggs and cook for 5 minutes, stirring frequently. Serves 3.

Cook's Notes:

POTATO CASSEROLE

Casseruola di Patate

6 medium (about 2 lbs.)   1 cup leaf lard
   potatoes, peeled and cut   Salt and pepper to taste
   into halves

Put potatoes in 2 qt. casserole. Dot with lard. Sprinkle with
salt and pepper. Bake uncovered at 350° for 45 to 60 minutes
or until crispy and golden brown. Serves 6.

Cook's Notes:

BAKED POTATO AND TOMATO

Patate e Pomodoro al Forno

1 tablespoon olive oil
4 medium potatoes, sliced
½ inch thick
4 medium tomatoes, sliced
4 medium onions, thinly
sliced
¼ cup Parmesan or
Romano cheese, grated

½ cup Provolone or Fontina
cheese, shredded
¼ teaspoon oregano
(optional)
1½ teaspoons salt
⅛ teaspoon pepper
¼ cup butter or olive oil

Grease casserole with 1 tablespoon oil. **Arrange** vegetables in layers. **Sprinkle** each layer with grated cheese, shredded Provolone, oregano, salt and pepper. **Repeat** until all ingredients are used. **Dot** with butter. **Bake** at 400° for 50 minutes or until vegetables are tender. Serves 4.

Cook's Notes:

CREAMY CHEESE POTATOES

Patate con Crema

6 medium potatoes, peeled
  and sliced
2 tablespoons butter
2 tablespoons flour
1 cup milk
¼ cup dry white wine
1 teaspoon salt

⅛ teaspoon pepper
⅛ teaspoon oregano or
  rosemary (optional)
1 cup (¼ lb.) Provolone
  cheese (mild, sharp or
  smoked), shredded

Place sliced potatoes in casserole. Melt butter in skillet. Stir
in flour to make smooth paste. Add milk and wine and bring to
boil, stirring constantly to prevent lumps. Add remaining ingredients and boil 2 minutes. Pour over potatoes. Bake at 350°
for 1 hour or until potatoes are tender, checking occasionally.
Serves 4–6.

Cook's Notes:

ROSEMARY'S POTATOES

Patate di Rosamaria

12 small (about 2 lbs.), new potatoes, peeled	1 teaspoon salt
½ cup butter or margarine	⅛ teaspoon pepper
½ cup oil	1 teaspoon rosemary, crushed

Soak potatoes in cold water for 20 minutes. **Drain** well and **place** in casserole. **Add** butter and oil. **Sprinkle** with salt, pepper and rosemary. **Bake** at 400° for 45 to 60 minutes or until crispy and tender. Serves 4–6.

VARIATION: *Roast potatoes*
Substitute 1 cup lard for butter and oil and omit rosemary.

Cook's Notes:

VEGETABLE CASSEROLE

Casseruola di Vegetali

2 tablespoons oil
1 lb. ground beef
6 potatoes, peeled and sliced
6 carrots, peeled and sliced
2 stalks celery, cut into ½-
   inch slices
2 large onions, sliced
1 4-oz. can sliced
   mushrooms, drained

Salt and pepper to taste
¼ cup Parmesan cheese,
   grated
1 lb. can peas, undrained
1 lb. can tomatoes
1 green pepper, sliced
   into rings

Heat oil in skillet over medium heat. **Brown** meat until it loses red color, breaking up with a fork (about 5 to 8 minutes). In 3-qt. casserole, **arrange** layers of potatoes, carrots, celery, onions, mushrooms and ground meat. **Sprinkle** with salt, pepper and grated cheese. **Pour** peas and tomatoes on top. **Garnish** with pepper rings. **Bake** at 350° for 1½ to 2 hours or until vegetables are tender. Can be prepared in advance and refrigerated. (If refrigerated, allow 15 more minutes for baking.) Serves 6.

Cook's Notes:

BAKED ZUCCHINI

Zucchini al Forno

2 large zucchini (each
  about ¾ lb., 2 inches in
  diameter, 8 inches long)
½ cup bread crumbs
Salt and pepper
½ teaspoon oregano,
  (optional)

¼ cup Parmesan cheese,
  grated
½ cup olive oil
1 clove garlic, minced
  (optional)

Wash zucchini and **trim off** stems. **Cut** in half lengthwise.
With a sharp knife, **cut** about 3 slits (¼ inch deep and ½ inch
apart) through open halves lengthwise and crosswise, so they
resemble checkerboards. Do not cut through skin. **Place** halves
in shallow baking pan. In small bowl **combine** bread crumbs,
salt, pepper and oregano. **Stir** with hand. **Sprinkle** each zucchini half with 2 tablespoons crumb mixture, 1 tablespoon grated
cheese, 2 tablespoons of oil and some garlic. **Bake** at 350° for
30 minutes or until tender when tested with fork. Serve hot or
cold. Serves 4.

VARIATION: Eggplant may be substituted for zucchini.

Serving suggestion: Serve with a crisp green salad and crusty
Italian bread.

Cook's Notes:

VENETIAN STYLE SQUASH

Zucchini alla Veneziana

3 zucchini (each about 2½ lbs., 2 inches in diameter, and 8 inches long)
1 slice white bread or 1 white roll
½ lb. ground beef
1 egg
1 slice prosciutto or ham
2 tablespoons Romano cheese, grated
1 clove garlic, minced or pressed
½ teaspoon salt
⅛ teaspoon pepper
2 tablespoons butter or half butter and half lard or bacon drippings
¼ cup onion, chopped
2 tablespoons parsley, chopped
2 tablespoons tomato paste
2 cups water
Salt and pepper

Wash zucchini, but do not peel. **Cut** ½ inch thick slice from ends and cut zucchini crosswise into thirds. **Scoop** out center of each piece with spoon or corer, leaving ½ inch thick wall. **Set** aside. (Pulp may be frozen and used in vegetable soup if not too seedy.) **Place** bread in small bowl. Add 1 cup water or enough to cover bread or roll. **Let** stand 2 minutes. **Remove** and **squeeze** dry. **Combine** bread with beef, egg, prosciutto or ham, cheese, garlic, salt and pepper. **Mix** well with hands. **Fill** zucchini and lay them on bottom of oval casserole. To make sauce **melt** butter in medium saucepan over medium heat. **Sauté** onion and parsley for 2 minutes, stirring often. **Add** remaining ingredients. **Stir** until well blended. **Bring** to boil. **Remove** from heat. Pour over zucchini. Can be frozen or refrigerated until ready to use. To serve immediately, **bake** at 350° about 45 to 55 minutes or until tender. (To test: pierce with fork.) **Check** from time to time, adding more water if necessary. Serve hot. Serves 4–5.

NOTE: If desired, **lift** cooked zucchini out of baking dish. **Place** in serving dish. **Strain** sauce and pour over 3 cups cooked rice (1 cup raw). **Sprinkle** with 2 tablespoons grated cheese. **Serve** hot.

VARIATIONS: *Zucchini alla Campania*
Prepare exactly as Venetian Style Squash, **omitting** sauce and last five ingredients. **Substitute** 2 cups tomato sauce or 2 8-oz. cans tomato sauce. (*See* Agrigento Eggplant Sauce, p. 167.) **Cook** in electric skillet or large skillet over low heat. **Bake** at 350° about 45 to 55 minutes or until tender when pierced with fork. Can be frozen.

With Brown Beef Gravy

1 cup **brown beef gravy**
(see below) or canned
1 cup **freshly made tomato**
sauce or 1 8-oz. can

⅛ teaspoon **nutmeg**
(optional)

Omit last 6 ingredients. **Substitute** above ingredients, mixed well. **Pour** over stuffed zucchini. Proceed as for Venetian Style Squash.

Brown Gravy

1 tablespoon **butter**
1 tablespoon **flour**

2 cups **brown beef stock or**
undiluted canned beef
bouillon

Melt butter in saucepan over low heat. **Add** flour. **Cook** 3 or 4 minutes or until lightly brown, stirring constantly. **Add** stock or bouillon. **Simmer** 5 minutes, stirring constantly until smooth. **Strain** if lumpy. **Cover** and refrigerate or freeze until needed. Makes about 1¾ cups.

Cook's Notes:

SQUASH WITH VEAL

Vitello con Zucchini

4 zucchini, 1–2 inches wide,
  6 inches long (about 2
  lbs.)
¼ cup olive or salad oil
2 medium onions, thinly
  sliced
1 ⚹2 can (2½ cups)
  fresh tomatoes, peeled
  and chopped
½ teaspoon oregano, or 4
  fresh basil leaves, or ½
  teaspoon dried basil

1 teaspoon salt
⅛ teaspoon pepper or to
  taste
2 tablespoons oil (more if
  necessary)
4 shoulder veal chops ½
  inch thick (about 2 lbs.)
Salt and pepper to taste
¼ cup Parmesan cheese
  grated (optional)

Wash zucchini and cut ⅛ inch off both ends. Cut zucchini
into 1-inch cubes and set aside. Heat oil in deep saucepan over
medium heat. Sauté onions, stirring constantly until soft (1 to 2
minutes). Add zucchini and cook until lightly brown (about 5
minutes), stirring occasionally. Add tomatoes and oregano or
basil. Cover tightly and steam 5 minutes. Heat 2 tablespoons oil
in skillet. (Add more oil if necessary.) Sauté chops on both sides
over medium fire (about 6 minutes for each side.) Sprinkle with
salt and pepper. When chops are brown but not done place
them in 2 qt. casserole or 12″×8″×3″ oblong casserole. Pour
zucchini mixture over meat. Sprinkle with cheese. Can be frozen.
To serve, bake at 375° for 45 minutes or until meat is fork-
tender. Check after 30 minutes. Some types of veal cook in less
time. Serves 4.

NOTE: To vary, both oregano and basil can be used or 1 Italian
green squash (cucuzza) for zucchini.

VARIATION: *Lamb Shanks with Zucchini*

Substitute 4 lamb shanks (about 3 lbs.) for veal. Have butcher saw through the shanks and tear off skin. **Heat** 1 tablespoon instead of ¼ cup oil in Dutch oven, deep heavy saucepan, or electric skillet. **Brown** shanks on all sides (15 to 20 minutes), turning frequently. **Drain off** excess fat and **bake** as above. (For extra flavor add crushed clove of garlic to browning onions.)

Cook's Notes:

FRIED SQUASH CASSEROLE

Casseruola con Zucchini Fritti

4 medium zucchini (about 1 lb.)
¼ cup flour
Salt and pepper
¼ cup olive oil or salad oil
¼ teaspoon oregano

1 small onion, minced
2 tablespoons Parmesan cheese, grated
1 cup tomato sauce or 1 8-oz. can tomato sauce

Wash zucchini; trim off ends, but do not peel. Cut into ¼-inch slices crosswise. In a paper bag, shake zucchini and flour seasoned with salt and pepper. Heat oil in large skillet over medium flame. Brown zucchini slices about 2 minutes on each side. Remove and arrange layer in 2-qt. casserole. Sprinkle with oregano, onion, cheese and sauce. Repeat process until all ingredients are used. Can be frozen or kept in refrigerator until ready to use. To serve, bake uncovered in preheated oven at 350° for 30 minutes or until tender when tested with fork. Serve hot or cold. Serves 4.

VARIATION: *Squash with Mozzarella or Fontina*
Omit oregano and onion. Add ½ lb. mozzarella or Fontina cheese, thinly sliced. Top layers of sauce with layers of cheese, ending with cheese.

Cook's Notes:

STEAMED SQUASH
Zucchini

3 firm, straight zucchini, ½
   lb. each
¼ cup olive oil or salad oil
2 scallions or small onions,
   chopped
3 medium potatoes (1 lb.)
   peeled and cut into 1-inch
   cubes

1 large ripe tomato (or 2
   small tomatoes), coarsely
   diced
4 fresh basil leaves or ¼
   teaspoon dried basil
   (optional)
Salt and pepper to taste

Wash zucchini, scrape lightly with potato peeler or knife.
Trim both ends of zucchini. Cut into 1-inch pieces. Heat oil in
large saucepan over medium fire. Add scallions or onions and
stir for a few seconds. Add potatoes and sauté 5 minutes stirring
constantly. Add zucchini and remaining ingredients. Cover
tightly, reduce heat to low, and steam vegetables for about 20
minutes or until tender, stirring occasionally. If necessary add
hot water. Can be frozen uncooked omitting potatoes. Serves 4.

VARIATION: Substitute 1 or 2 cups nested vermicelli or egg
noodles for potatoes. Add during last 6 minutes of cooking. Stir
and serve hot. If desired stir in 2 tablespoons grated cheese. Light
green Italian squash may be substituted if using noodles. Can be
frozen. (Freeze uncooked, without noodles.)

Cook's Notes:

STUFFED ZUCCHINI SICILIAN STYLE

Zucchini Ripieni all Siciliana

4 straight zucchini
1 tablespoon onion, chopped
1 tablespoon parsley, chopped
4 anchovy fillets, chopped
1 small fresh tomato, peeled and chopped

½ cup bread crumbs
Salt and pepper
6 tablespoons olive or salad oil
½ cup hot water
1 clove garlic, minced

Wash zucchini and trim stems but do not peel. **Cut** in halves lengthwise. With teaspoon **scoop** out pulp, leaving a ½-inch shell. **Set aside** shells, **dice** pulp and put in bowl. **Mix** in onion, parsley, anchovies, tomato, bread crumbs, salt (use salt sparingly as anchovies are salty), pepper and 2 tablespoons oil. **Mix** well and **fill** shells. **Place** in oblong casserole or shallow baking dish greased with 2 tablespoons oil. **Add** water and garlic to bottom of casserole or pan. **Sprinkle** with remaining oil. **Bake** uncovered at 350° for 30 to 45 minutes or until tender when pierced with fork. **Check** from time to time, adding more water if necessary. Serve hot or cold. May be frozen. Serves 4.

VARIATIONS: *With Mushrooms*
   Add ½ cup (about 6 medium) chopped fresh mushrooms to pulp mixture.

With Mushrooms and Capers
   Add ½ cup chopped mushrooms and 2 teaspoons capers to pulp mixture.

With Prosciutto or Salami
   Substitute 3 slices chopped prosciutto or salami for anchovies.

Egg Filling

Omit anchovies and tomatoes. **Substitute** 1 egg, ¼ cup grated Italian cheese and an additional ½ cup bread crumbs.

With Herbs

Add ¼ teaspoon oregano, or 4 fresh chopped basil leaves or ¼ teaspoon dried basil.

Cook's Notes:

ZUCCHINI AND EGGPLANT

Zucchini e Melanzane Gratinate

2 medium (about 1 lb.)
  zucchini
1 (about 1 lb.) eggplant,
  peeled or unpeeled, cut
  into 1-inch cubes
6 tablespoons oil or salad oil
1 large onion, finely
  chopped

1 clove garlic, minced
  (optional)
¼ lb. fresh mushrooms,
  sliced
1 tablespoon parsley, minced
¼ cup fine bread crumbs
Salt and pepper to taste

Wash zucchini thoroughly. **Cut** into 1-inch cubes. **Heat** 2 tablespoons oil in frying pan over medium fire. **Sauté** zucchini until tender (about 10 minutes), stirring frequently. **Remove** from skillet and place in bowl. **Heat** 2 tablespoons oil in same skillet. **Sauté** eggplant until lightly brown and tender (about 10 minutes), stirring often. If necessary, add more oil. **Remove** and add to zucchini. **Heat** remaining oil in same skillet. **Stir** in onion and garlic and **sauté** until soft (about 2 to 3 minutes). **Add** mushrooms and cook 5 minutes, stirring occasionally. **Stir** in parsley, bread crumbs, salt and pepper. Cook 1 minute longer. Spread over zucchini and eggplant. Serves 4–6.

Cook's Notes:

SQUASH WITH HAM

Zucchini con Prosciutto

8 small zucchini, 1 inch in diameter, 5 inches long
10 cups salted water or to cover
2 small onions or 1 bunch small green onions, minced
2 tablespoons parsley, minced

2 slices bacon, diced
4 slices prosciutto or ham, diced
4 tablespoons butter ($\frac{1}{2}$ stick)
Salt and pepper

Wash zucchini and **cut off** stems. **Drop** into boiling water salted with 1 teaspoon of salt for 2 minutes. **Drain** and **cool.** Cut in halves lengthwise. **Tear off** 3-foot length of 18 inch wide broiling foil, fold in half. **Turn up** sides to form pouch. **Place** zucchini cut-side up in foil. **Mix** onions, parsley, bacon, and prosciutto or ham. **Sprinkle** over zucchini. **Dot** with butter. Sprinkle lightly with salt (ham is salty) and pepper. **Seal** securely. **Place** on grill over hot coals. **Grill** about 20 to 30 minutes, turning once. To **test,** pinch squash; if soft it is cooked. (Cooking time will vary with heat.) **Unwrap** carefully to save juices. Serve from package. Can be frozen. (Bake at 350° for 45 minutes to unthaw and cook.) Serves 4.

Cook's Notes:

SQUASH STEW

Zucchini Stufato

4 medium (or 6 small) zucchini
¼ cup oil
1 medium onion, sliced
3 fresh tomatoes, peeled and chopped

1 teaspoon salt or to taste
⅛ teaspoon pepper
½ bay leaf
2 fresh basil leaves or
  ⅛ teaspoon dried basil
  (optional)

Wash zucchini and **trim off** ends. **Cut** into 1-inch cubes. **Heat** oil in large skillet over medium heat. **Add** zucchini and onion. **Sauté** over low fire for 5 minutes, stirring frequently. **Add** remaining ingredients. **Cover** and **cook** 15 to 20 minutes or until squash is tender when pierced with fork, stirring occasionally. Add more water if necessary.

VARIATION: *With Green Peppers*
  To the above recipe **add** 2 green peppers, pitted, and sliced lengthwise in eighths. **Sauté** pepper with zucchini and onions. **Omit** bay leaf and basil.

With Mushrooms and Green Peppers
  Use ¼ lb. fresh sliced mushrooms and 2 green peppers, pitted and sliced lengthwise into eighths. **Sauté** mushrooms and pepper with zucchini and onions. **Omit** bay leaf and basil.

Cook's Notes:

Eggplant

This very popular, shiny pear or egg-shaped purple fruit is known as "La Melanzana." It is really a fruit but is used in cooking as a vegetable. Eggplants vary in length from 6 to 12 inches. Good eggplants should be heavy and firm and of uniform size. Select a smooth, glossy purple eggplant; a wrinkled eggplant is old and will have a bitter flavor. Small and medium eggplants are best; large ones are apt to be pitted. A medium eggplant weighs about 1½ lbs. and serves 4–6. A small size (about ½ lb.) is just right for stuffing. Very small eggplants (about the size of an egg or a lemon) have a more distinct and delicate flavor than larger eggplants. Eggplant can be broiled, fried, baked, stuffed, pickled, and combined in many casseroles.

Preparing Eggplant

1. Wash eggplant but don't peel unless the skin is tough. Eggplant discolors quickly when cut and should be sprinkled or rubbed with lemon juice. Cover with a plate and a weight. Let stand at least 1 hour, then drain off the resulting brown liquid; rinse and dry on paper towels to absorb excess moisture.

2. Eggplant has a blotter-like capacity for oil or butter. In cooking, heat the oil until it is very hot but not smoky to prevent excess oil absorption.

3. Eggplant takes on intriguing flavor with the addition of numerous spices.

4. Eggplant and tomatoes combine to make hearty casseroles. Sliced or diced leftover meats or fish make a complete one-dish meal.

5. Eggplant is excellent when braised with meats; it can also be served as an appetizer and included in numerous casserole dishes.

6. Eggplant can be used in a green salad or sprinkled generously on soup.

7. Eggplant makes beautiful individual servings when stuffed. Try alternating stuffed eggplants with green and red stuffed peppers for an effective buffet platter.

AGRIGENTO EGGPLANT

Melanzana alla Agrigento

2 medium eggplants
2 teaspoons salt
3–4 eggs (as needed)
2 cups bread crumbs
¼ teaspoon salt
⅛ teaspoon pepper
1 tablespoon parsley,
   minced

1¼ cups salad oil (more if
   necessary)
1 cup Parmesan cheese,
   grated
½ lb. mozzarella or
   Provolone cheese, thinly
   sliced
Tomato sauce (see below)

Wash eggplant and slice crosswise into ¼-inch slices. **Sprinkle** with salt, and **place** in colander, let stand for 30 minutes. **Squeeze** each slice dry with palms of hands. **Heat** oil in large skillet over medium fire until very hot. (Oil should be ½ inch deep.) **Dip** each slice in beaten eggs, then into crumbs combined with salt, pepper and parsley. **Fry** in hot oil until golden brown on each side (about 3 minutes). Add more oil if necessary. **Drain** on paper towel or brown paper. **Spread** ⅓ of tomato sauce onto bottom of 10–12 inch (2 qt.) casserole, or 13″×9″×2″ baking dish. **Spread** layer of eggplant slices and **sprinkle** with grated Parmesan cheese. **Top** with layer of mozzarella or Provolone cheese. **Repeat** layers until all ingredients are used, ending with slices of mozzarella or Provolone cheese. Can be frozen. To serve immediately, **bake** at 400° for 15 minutes or until cheese begins to melt and is slightly brown, and sauce is bubbly. Serves 4–6.

Sauce

2 tablespoons oil	Salt and pepper to taste
1 clove garlic	1 teaspoon sugar (optional)
1 tablespoon onion, minced	¼ teaspoon dried basil or 4
2 6-oz. cans tomato paste	fresh basil leaves
5 cups water	

Heat oil in Dutch oven or large saucepan over medium fire. **Sauté** garlic and onion 2 minutes or until soft. Discard garlic if desired. **Stir in** tomato paste, water, salt, pepper, sugar and basil. **Bring** to boiling, then simmer uncovered 45 minutes or until thick, stirring often.

NOTE: If you are fond of herbs, add 1 teaspoon oregano to sauce.

VARIATIONS: *With Fresh Tomatoes*

In summer when tomatoes are plentiful, **substitute** them for tomato paste. **Omit** water and **cut** unpeeled tomatoes into quarters or eighths. **Place** in saucepan about 4 lbs. ripe fresh tomatoes and **cook** covered over medium fire until soft (about 20 minutes). **Press** through sieve or place in blender. **Cook** 30 minutes instead of 45 minutes, stirring constantly until thick.

With Ground Beef

Add 1 lb. ground beef to Dutch oven or saucepan after garlic and onion are sautéed. **Brown** meat until red color disappears (about 5 minutes), stirring with fork to break up meat. **Spoon** off excess fat.

Serving suggestion: Serve with zesty green salad, crusty Italian bread, and a fruit dessert.

Cook's Notes:

EGGPLANT WITH ANCHOVY

Melanzana con Acciughe

2 small (about 1 lb. each)
eggplants
2 tablespoons olive oil
1 medium onion, chopped
1 medium fresh tomato,
peeled and chopped, or
½ cup canned tomatoes
16 green olives, pitted and
sliced
½ cup bread crumbs

6 anchovy fillets, chopped
2 tablespoons capers
1 teaspoon parsley, chopped
⅛ teaspoon dried basil or 1
fresh basil leaf (optional)
Salt and pepper
3 tablespoons oil
1 cup tomato-meat sauce,
plain sauce or 1 8-oz. can
tomato sauce

Wash and **dry** eggplants. **Cut** in halves lengthwise. With teaspoon, carefully **scoop out** inside pulp, leaving shell about ½-inch thick. **Dice** pulp and **set aside**. **Heat** oil in skillet over medium fire. **Sauté** onion 2 minutes and stir. **Add** pulp and tomatoes. **Sauté** 5 minutes, stirring constantly. **Remove** from heat and **stir in** olives, bread crumbs, anchovies, capers, parsley and basil. **Season** with salt and pepper. (Use salt very sparingly as anchovies are salty.) **Fill** shells. **Grease** baking dish with 1 tablespoon of oil. **Place** pieces of eggplant close together so they will hold their shape. **Pour** sauce over eggplant. **Sprinkle** with remaining oil. Bake at 375° for 30 minutes. When ready to serve, lift up with pancake turner. Can be frozen. Serves 4–5.

Cook's Notes:

EGGPLANT CALABRIA

Melanzana alla Calabria

6 small (3–4 inches long)   2 cloves garlic, crushed
    eggplants   ½ teaspoon oregano
½ cup olive oil   Salt and pepper

Cut off stem end of eggplants and wash. Cut in halves lengthwise. Make crisscross cuts about 1½ inches deep on pulp of eggplant halves. Place in greased shallow baking dish. Mix oil and
garlic and brush half over cut side of eggplants. Sprinkle with
oregano, salt and pepper. Drizzle with remaining oil mixture.
Bake uncovered at 375° for ½ to 1 hour (depending on size of
eggplant), or until tender when tested with fork. If too dry during cooking brush on more oil. Serves 4–6.

VARIATION: Cut 2 medium tomatoes into ½ inch slices. Place
sliced tomatoes on top of eggplant.

Cook's Notes:

EGGPLANT WITH CAPERS

Melanzana con Capperi

1 medium eggplant (about 1½ lbs.), cut into 1-inch cubes
¼ cup olive oil
1 8-oz. can tomato sauce or 3 medium fresh ripe tomatoes, peeled and diced
12 black olives, pitted and sliced
12 capers
Salt and pepper to taste

Heat oil in skillet or casserole over medium fire. **Add** eggplant and cook until light brown and tender (about 10 minutes), stirring often. Add more oil if necessary. **Stir in** tomato sauce or fresh tomatoes, olives and capers. **Sprinkle** with salt and pepper to taste. **Cover** and **cook** 5 minutes, **uncover** and **cook** 5 minutes longer. Serve hot or cold. Can be frozen. (Freeze slightly undercooked.) Serves 4.

VARIATION: **Add** 1 clove minced garlic and ½ teaspoon of oregano to hot oil.

Serving Suggestion: Serve with escarole salad and Italian bread. This makes a delicious sandwich filling.

Cook's Notes:

EGGPLANT PALERMO

Melanzana alla Palermitana

6 very small (about 3–4
inches long) eggplants,
unpeeled
2 cloves garlic, chopped
6 fresh basil leaves, chopped,
or 1 teaspoon dry basil
¼ cup olive oil

1 ⅜2½ can tomato purée
Salt and pepper to taste
1 lb. elbow, ditali, Mafalda
(curly long macaroni) or
any long macaroni
¼ cup grated cheese

Cut off stem ends of eggplants and wash. Make 4 1½-inch
slits lengthwise on each eggplant. Do not cut all the way to ends
or eggplant will break apart. Insert some of garlic and basil in
each slit. Heat oil in Dutch oven or large saucepan over medium
heat. Sauté eggplant for 10 minutes, turning frequently. Add
tomato purée, salt and pepper. Cover and simmer 1 hour or
until tender when tested with a fork. Can be frozen at this point.

Cook macaroni as directed on package label until chewy
(*al dente*). Drain and place in 3-qt. casserole or serving dish.
Add small amount of tomato sauce. Toss with two forks and
keep adding sauce until well-coated but not soupy. Serve in
individual dishes. Top with 1 or more eggplants. Pass remaining
sauce and grated Parmesan cheese. (Sauce can be prepared in
advance.) Serves 6.

VARIATION: *With Eggs*
Add 6 eggs during last 10 minutes of cooking. Break eggs on
edge of pan and drop in one at a time. Do not stir. Cook 10
minutes or until egg whites are firm. Serve with large spoon.

EGGPLANT CATANZARO STYLE

Melanzana alla Catanzaro

2 eggplants (about 1 lb.
   each) unpeeled and cut
   crosswise into ¼-inch
   slices
1 lb. ground beef
¼ cup Parmesan or
   Romano cheese, grated
½ cup bread crumbs
¼ cup onion, minced

1 tablespoon basil or
   parsley, finely chopped
1 egg
1 teaspoon salt
⅛ teaspoon pepper
¼ cup olive oil or salad oil
2 cups meatless tomato
   sauce

In medium bowl, **combine** meat, cheese, bread crumbs, onion, basil or parsley, egg, salt and pepper. **Mix** thoroughly with hands. **Spread** generous tablespoon of mixture on 1 side of eggplant slice. **Cover** with another slice to form sandwich. **Secure** with toothpick, if necessary. **Continue** until all eggplant slices and meat mixture have been used. **Heat** oil in large frying pan over medium fire. **Brown** eggplant sandwiches about 4 minutes on each side, turning carefully. Add more oil if necessary. **Put** film of sauce in bottom of casserole or baking dish. **Place** eggplant over sauce and **top** with more sauce. (Can be frozen or refrigerated until ready to use.) **Bake** in preheated oven at 350° for about 45 minutes or until eggplant is soft. **Lift** sandwiches with pancake turner. Serves 6.

VARIATIONS: 1. **Use** 12 small eggplants about 3 inches long, instead of larger eggplants. **Wash** and **cut off** top stems. With a sharp knife or grapefruit knife, **scoop out** inside pulp, leaving a shell about ¼ inch thick. Handle very carefully so they will not break apart. **Fill** each eggplant shell with meat mixture.

2. **Place** half of raw eggplant slices in greased casserole or baking dish. **Spread** generous tablespoon of meat mixture on one side of half of eggplant slices. **Cover** with remaining eggplant slice to form sandwiches.

Cook's Notes:

EGGPLANT AND LAMB CASSEROLE
Pasticcio

6 shoulder lamb chops,
  ½ inch thick
3 tablespoons olive oil
4 medium (about 1 lb.)
  fresh tomatoes, thinly
  sliced
1½ teaspoons salt
¼ teaspoon black pepper
4 fresh basil leaves or ¼
  teaspoon dried basil
1 medium (about 1½ lbs.)
eggplant, peeled and cut
  crosswise into ¼-inch
  slices
2 medium green peppers,
  cut lengthwise into eighths
1 cup uncooked Italian rice
  or regular rice
1 10½-oz. can (about 1¼
  cups) tomato purée
1 tablespoon olive oil

Heat oil in skillet over medium heat. Brown chops about 4 minutes on each side. Remove and set aside. In bottom of 3-qt. casserole spread half the tomatoes. Sprinkle with salt, pepper and basil. Add half the eggplant and green pepper slices. Sprinkle each layer with salt, pepper and basil. Repeat layers. Combine rice and tomato purée. Pour over layers. Sprinkle with oil. Place browned chops on rice. Season with salt and pepper. Cover tightly and bake at 350° until meat is tender (about 1½ hours). Uncover and cook 10 minutes longer. Can be prepared in advance and frozen. Serves 6.

NOTE: *Pasticciare* literally means "mixup dish" or culinary pastiche. Can be expanded with potatoes, string beans, zucchini or mushrooms.

VARIATION: Substitute 1 lb. ground beef for lamb chops. Cook meat until lightly brown, breaking up with fork. If desired, add 1 medium onion, chopped, with the ground beef. Proceed as above.

Serving Suggestion: Serve with crusty Italian bread and green salad.

Cook's Notes:

EGGPLANT PEASANT STYLE

Melanzana alla Paesana

Fried eggplant (see p. 178)
¼ cup olive oil
1 medium onion, thinly
    sliced
1 ⚹3 can tomatoes

Salt and pepper to taste
¼ cup ricotta cheese,
    grated, or Italian cheese

Heat oil in skillet over medium high flame. **Sauté** onion until soft (about 3 minutes), stirring occasionally. **Mash** tomatoes with back of spoon or fork or squeeze with hands. **Stir** into onion. **Cook** uncovered 20 minutes, stirring frequently. While sauce is cooking, **prepare** eggplant. As eggplant slices become browned, remove to dish. When all slices are fried, **alternate** layers of eggplant, cheese and sauce in serving dish or casserole. Can be frozen. (If freezing, sauté eggplant slices for only 3 minutes.) **Bake** uncovered at 375° for 30 to 45 minutes or until sauce is bubbly. Check after 30 minutes. Serve hot or cold. Serves 4–6.

NOTE: Excellent for sandwiches.

VARIATIONS: *With Meat*

Sauté ½ lb. ground beef with onion until meat loses its red color, breaking up meat with fork as it cooks. **Proceed** as above.

With Zucchini

Substitute 2 medium zucchini (about 8 inches long and 2 inches in diameter) for eggplant. **Wash** and scrape skin slightly. **Cut** crosswise into ¼-inch slices. **Fry** in ¼ cup olive oil over medium heat until lightly browned and soft (about 3 minutes on each side). Can be frozen.

EGGPLANT PARMESAN

Melanzana alla Parmigiana

1 large (or 2 medium)
eggplant
Plain tomato sauce (see p.
224)
1½ cups bread crumbs
1 teaspoon salt
⅛ teaspoon pepper

¼ teaspoon dried basil or 4
fresh basil leaves
2 eggs, slightly beaten
½ cup oil (more if
necessary)
½ lb. mozzarella cheese,
diced
1 cup Parmesan cheese,
grated

Wash eggplant and slice crosswise into ¼-inch slices. Sprinkle about ⅛ teaspoon salt on each layer of eggplant and place in colander for about 1 hour. Prepare sauce. Rinse eggplant in cold water and drain.

In large bowl, combine bread crumbs, salt, pepper and basil. Blend. Dip slices of eggplant in beaten eggs, then in seasoned crumbs. Heat oil in skillet. Brown eggplant 3 minutes on one side over medium fire. Turn and brown other side 2 minutes. Remove and set aside. Spread ⅓ of sauce on bottom of 2 qt. casserole or 12″×8″×2″ baking pan. Over this arrange layer of eggplant, then ⅓ of mozzarella cheese. Sprinkle with Parmesan cheese. Spread with layer of sauce. Repeat layers until all ingredients are used up, ending with sauce. Bake 20 to 25 minutes at 350° or until mozzarella is bubbly and some of sauce has been absorbed. Can be prepared ahead of time. Serves 5–6.

Cook's Notes:

SICILIAN FRIED EGGPLANT

Melanzana Fritta alla Siciliana

2 medium (about 1 lb.   Pepper
  each) or 1 large eggplant   ¼ cup Parmesan cheese,
2 teaspoons salt   grated
1 cup salad oil (more if
  necessary)

Wash eggplant, and slice crosswise into ¼-inch slices. **Sprinkle** with salt and **let stand** 5 minutes in colander. **Squeeze** dry with palms of hands. **Heat** oil in large frying pan over medium fire. **Fry** eggplant slices in hot oil until golden brown on both sides (about 6 to 8 minutes). As eggplant slices are completed, **arrange** in layers on serving platter. Sprinkle each slice with pepper and cheese. **Repeat.** Serve hot or cold. (To freeze, fry slices for 2 minutes on each side. To serve, thaw and fry 2 more minutes on each side.) Serves 4–6.

NOTE: Makes excellent sandwich filling.

Cook's Notes:

EGGPLANT AND VEGETABLE CASSEROLE

Melanzana Vegetali al Forno

1 medium eggplant (about 1 lb.), unpeeled and cut into 1-inch cubes

2 zucchini (about ½ lb. each), washed and cut into 1-inch cubes

¼ cup olive oil (more if necessary)

2 medium onions, thinly sliced

2 green peppers or sweet red peppers, seeded and sliced into 1-inch strips

½ lb. fresh mushrooms, sliced (optional)

Salt and pepper to taste

3 medium fresh tomatoes, peeled and cut into eighths or 1 cup canned Italian plum tomatoes

3 tablespoons parsley, minced (optional)

Heat oil in large frying pan over medium fire. Sauté eggplant and zucchini until lightly browned and soft (about 8 to 10 minutes) turning occasionally. Remove to dish and set aside. Add 2 to 3 tablespoons more oil if necessary and cook onions, pepper and mushrooms 5 minutes or until soft, stirring frequently. Season with salt and pepper. Add tomatoes, cover pan and cook 5 minutes. Stir in parsley. Spoon half of tomato mixture into bottom of 3 qt. (2½" deep) casserole or Dutch oven. Arrange eggplant and zucchini over tomato mixture. Cover with remaining tomato mixture. Can be frozen or refrigerated. Can be served hot or cold. To serve hot, cover casserole and cook 10 minutes over low heat. Uncover. If too juicy, tip casserole and pour out some of juices. Serves 4–6.

Cook's Notes:

EGGPLANT STEW

Melanzana Ciambotta

1 medium (about 1½ lbs.) eggplant, peeled and cut into 1–1½ inch cubes
¼ cup olive oil
1 clove garlic
2 medium onions, thinly sliced and separated into rings
4 medium green peppers, stems and seeds removed, cut into eighths
7–8 medium fresh ripe tomatoes, peeled and chopped, or 4 cups canned tomatoes
1 lb. fresh peas, shelled (preferred) or 1 10-oz. package frozen peas
1 lb. fresh string beans, ends snipped off and cut into halves (preferred), or 2 10-oz. packages frozen string beans
8 green olives, pitted and sliced
8 black olives, pitted and sliced
2 medium potatoes, peeled and cut into 1½-inch cubes
1 bay leaf, or 4 fresh basil leaves or ¼ teaspoon dried basil
Salt and pepper

Heat oil in Dutch oven or large, deep heavy pot over medium fire. **Add** garlic and **sauté** until golden brown stirring frequently (about 1 minute). Discard if desired. **Sauté** onions until soft (about 2 minutes), stirring constantly. **Add** green peppers. **Cover** and **steam** about 6 to 7 minutes or until soft. **Add** tomatoes. **Cover** and **cook** 15 minutes longer, stirring often. **Stir** in remaining ingredients. **Cover** and **reduce** heat to low. **Cook** 30 minutes or until vegetables are tender. Serve hot or cold. Can be frozen, omitting potatoes. (Cook vegetables for only five minutes before freezing.) Serves 4–6.

Serving suggestion: Serve with crispy garlic bread and a fresh fruit and cheese dessert.

VARIATION: *Eggplant Hero Sandwich*

1 loaf crusty Italian bread, about 20 inches long	3 slices mozzarella cheese Eggplant Stew

Cut bread lengthwise and fill with Eggplant Stew. Serve hot or cold. If desired cover with mozzarella cheese. Serves 3. (Two 12-inch loaves of bread, four 6-inch rolls or three 8-inch rolls may be used.)

Cook's Notes:

STUFFED EGGPLANT

Melanzana Ripiena

2 medium eggplants about
1½ lbs. each
2 tablespoons olive oil
1 small onion or 6 green
onion tops, minced
1 lb. ground beef, pork
or lamb
2 tablespoons parsley, finely
chopped

½ cup bread crumbs
1 teaspoon salt
⅛ teaspoon pepper or to
taste
2 tablespoons oil
1 ⚹10½ can (1¼ cups)
tomato purée or tomato
sauce

Wash and **dry** eggplants. **Cut** lengthwise into halves. With a
teaspoon, carefully **scoop out** inside pulp, leaving a shell about
½ inch thick. **Dice** pulp, and **set aside**. **Heat** oil in skillet over
medium fire. **Sauté** eggplant pulp, onion, meat and parsley for
5 minutes, stirring constantly. **Remove** from heat and **stir in**
bread crumbs, salt and pepper. **Fill** shells. **Grease** baking dish
with 1 tablespoon oil. **Place** eggplant halves close together so
they will retain shape. **Pour** tomato purée or sauce over eggplant
and **sprinkle** with remaining oil. **Bake** at 375° for 30 minutes.
When ready to serve lift with pancake turner. Can be frozen.
(Freeze before baking.) Serves 4–5.

NOTE: 2 cups leftover chopped cooked meat can be substituted for ground beef. Combine with bread crumbs and seasonings and add to sautéed vegetables. (A good way to use up
leftovers.)

VARIATIONS: **Substitute** 10 very small eggplants (3–4 inches
long) for 2 medium eggplants. **Wash** and **cut off** stem of each
eggplant. **Scoop** out pulp with knife or teaspoon, leaving a shell
about ¼ inch thick. **Fill** shells with stuffing mixture. **Heat** ¼ cup

oil in large frying pan. **Brown** eggplants on all sides (about 8 to 10 minutes), adding more oil if needed. Remove and **place** in saucepan; **cover** with sauce. **Simmer,** covered, over low heat for 20 minutes or until tender when tested with fork.

Stuffed Squash

Substitute 3 zucchini (about 1 lb. each and 2 inches in diameter and 8 inches long) for eggplant. Bake 20 minutes. Can be frozen before baking.

Cook's Notes:

WHITE EGGPLANT

Melanzana Bianca

1 medium (about 1½ lbs.)
    eggplant, peeled and
    sliced crosswise into
    ¼-inch slices
½ cup flour
½ teaspoon salt
¼ teaspoon pepper
2 eggs, beaten

½ cup oil
1 lb. (2 cups), ricotta or
    creamed cottage cheese
½ lb. mozzarella or
    Provolone cheese, thinly
    sliced
¼ cup Parmesan cheese,
    grated

Mix flour, salt and pepper in bowl. **Dip** each eggplant slice in flour and beaten egg. **Heat** oil in large frying pan over medium fire. **Fry** slices about 3 minutes on each side or until tender and golden brown. If necessary add more oil. **Remove** from pan and drain on paper towel. **Arrange** layer of eggplant in bottom of 2 qt. flameproof casserole or 12"×8"×2" baking dish. **Spread** ⅓ of ricotta over eggplant slices. **Cover** with mozzarella and **sprinkle** with grated cheese. **Repeat** layers until all ingredients are used. **Sprinkle** with oil. Can be frozen. **Bake** at 400° for 20 minutes or until mozzarella is bubbly and melted. (If frozen, bake at 375° for 50 or 60 minutes.) Serves 6.

VARIATIONS: *With Lasagne*
  Add layer of cooked lasagne (½ lb.).

With Meat Sauce
  Brown ¾ lb. ground beef in 1 tablespoon oil until it loses red color (about 5 minutes). **Stir** into tomato sauce. **Alternate** layers of eggplant and sauce.

Cook's Notes:

Artichokes

Fresh, plump artichokes are adaptable to many kinds of meals and perform a multitude of duties in any menu. They contribute a delectable flavor and colorful appearance in appetizers, soups, salads, or entrees. The silver-green artichoke, a member of the thistle family, grows along the coast of central California.

Cooking an artichoke is easier than eating one. To eat an artichoke, simply pluck away the leaves one or two at a time, draw the tender end between the teeth to scrape off the meaty portion at the base of the leaf, and discard the rest. The leaves nearest the center are the most tender. In the center is the heart, topped with a fuzzy crown. Remove the crown by slipping a fork or knife under it and cutting it from the base. The bottom part, the heart, is solid artichoke meat, and is considered the choicest part of the artichoke.

The *articiocco* became popular in the 15th century in Italy. In Italy today artichokes are stuffed with fresh mint, garlic and oil and steamed in the vapors of a dry white wine. They are also fried whole in oil or deep-fat fried until the leaves curl and the plant opens like a flower. To reproduce these delights, one must have available small artichokes with the chokes still undeveloped.

Preparing Artichoke Shells

1. Wash each artichoke under cold running water.

2. Pull off tough outer leaves, working from base to top and discard.

3. Hold artichoke on its side. With a sharp knife, cut off about 1 inch straight across the top.

4. Cut off stem even with base, so that artichoke will stand upright in pan.

5. Place artichoke cut side down on cutting board or a flat surface. With palm of hand, firmly press down on base to open leaves. Then spread leaves apart to make well or cup in center.

6. Pull out yellow center leaves. (Beware of needle-sharp tips.) With spoon or paring knife scrape out choke (thistle-like hairy mass on bottom).

7. Add one tablespoon red wine, vinegar or lemon juice per

quart to cooking water to prevent discoloration, or rub cut side with vinegar or lemon, or spread with oil.

8. Artichoke is now ready for stuffing, boiling or slicing. May be frozen until ready to use.

Freezing Stuffed Artichokes

Put 4 qts. water and juice of 2 lemons in large kettle over high fire. Bring to rolling boil. Add artichokes one by one and bring to rolling boil again. Cover tightly and turn off heat. Let stand 4 minutes without lifting cover. Cool heated artichokes under cold running water or plunge in pan of ice cold water 5 minutes. Set artichokes upside down on paper towels to drain.

Stuff with filling. Place each artichoke in center of 12″ square of aluminum freezing foil. Bring the foil up to form cup and twist foil over top. Freeze.

To serve, unwrap frozen artichokes and place upright in saucepan with 1 inch water. Cover and cook over medium fire 45 to 60 minutes or until an outer leaf can be easily pulled, adding a little more water if needed.

ARTICHOKES WITH WINE

Carciofi con Vino

6 small artichokes
2 cloves garlic, minced
½ cup parsley, minced
4 fresh mint leaves or ¼
  teaspoon dried mint,
  crushed

Salt and pepper to taste
¼ cup olive oil
½ cup chicken broth, fresh
  or canned
1 cup sauterne or any white
  wine

Prepare artichokes as directed for artichoke shells. In bowl **mix** together garlic, parsley, mint, salt and pepper. **Divide** into 6 parts. **Fill** center of each artichoke. **Place** upright in deep saucepan or casserole. (Artichokes should fit snugly to prevent spreading.) **Pour** oil over them. **Cook** over low fire 10 minutes. **Add** broth and wine. **Cover** tightly and **cook** over low fire about 25 to 35 minutes or until tender. Add more broth or wine if necessary. To **test,** pull an outer leaf; if it comes off easily it is done. Can be frozen. Serves 4.

Cook's Notes:

CHICKEN LIVERS WITH ARTICHOKES

Fegato di Pollo con Carciofi

8 small tender artichokes or
1 package 9-oz. frozen
artichoke hearts, thawed
1 qt. cold water
Juice of ½ lemon
3 tablespoons olive oil
½ teaspoon salt
⅛ teaspoon pepper
4 tablespoons butter or
margarine

1 lb. chicken livers
⅛ teaspoon rosemary
(optional)
2 slices prosciutto or bacon,
cut into ½-inch pieces
1 tablespoon parsley, minced
Juice of ½ lemon

Wash fresh artichokes under cold running water. **Pull off** tough outer leaves, working from base to top. With sharp knife **slice** 1 inch off top, cutting straight across. **Cut** stems even with base. With scissors, **cut off** thorny tips. **Cut** lengthwise into halves. **Scoop out** choke (fuzzy center) with spoon or paring knife. **Slice** each half into 4 slices. **Drop** into bowl containing 1 qt. water and lemon juice (to retain color) for 15 minutes. **Drain. Place** oil and artichokes in skillet over medium fire or in electric skillet. **Sprinkle** with salt and pepper. **Fry** 15 to 20 minutes or until brown and tender, stirring occasionally. If artichokes seem too dry during cooking add water. While artichokes are cooking, **melt** butter in saucepan over medium fire. **Add** chicken livers and **sprinkle** with rosemary. **Cook** 7 minutes or until livers are tender, stirring constantly. **Mix** prosciutto or bacon with chicken livers. **Combine** with artichokes. **Cook** over medium fire 2 minutes, stirring constantly. **Sprinkle** with parsley and lemon juice. Serve hot. Can be frozen. Serves 4.

LATIUM CHICKEN BREAST
AND ARTICHOKES

Petti di Pollo alla Lazio

2 whole (about 2½ to 3 lbs.) chicken breasts
4 tablespoons butter or half butter and half olive oil
3 small onions, sliced into ⅛-inch rings
1 9-oz. pkg. frozen artichokes, thawed
¼ lb. fresh small whole mushrooms, or 1 4-oz. can mushrooms, drained
Salt and pepper to taste
½ to ¾ cup chicken broth, fresh or canned

Bone chicken and **cut** into 1-inch cubes. **Heat** butter or butter and oil in large skillet over medium fire or in electric skillet. **Add** chicken and cook until white (about 3 to 5 minutes), stirring constantly. **Add** onions separated into rings, artichokes and mushrooms. **Sprinkle** with salt and pepper. **Stir** in ½ cup broth. **Cook** 7 to 10 minutes or until chicken and vegetables are tender. Add more broth if needed. Can be frozen. Serves 4–6.

Serving suggestion: Serve with buttered rice, Italian bread and tray of fruit.

Cook's Notes:

BAKED ARTICHOKES
TUSCAN STYLE
Tortina di Carciofi

6 small tender artichokes or
  2 9-oz. packages frozen
  artichoke hearts, thawed
1 qt. water
Juice of 1 lemon
4 tablespoons flour
1 cup oil

6 eggs
¼ cup milk or light cream
⅛ teaspoon nutmeg
2 tablespoons Romano
  cheese, grated (optional)
Salt and pepper to taste

Wash fresh artichokes under cold running water. **Pull off** tough outer leaves, working from base to top. With sharp knife **slice** 1 inch off top, cutting straight across. **Cut** stems even with base. With scissors, **cut off** thorny tips. **Cut** lengthwise into halves. **Scoop out** choke (fuzzy center) with spoon or paring knife. **Slice** each half into 8 to 10 thin slices. **Drop** into bowl containing 1 qt. water and lemon juice. When artichokes are all sliced **drain** them and **dry** with paper towel. **Roll** in flour. **Heat** oil in skillet over medium fire. **Fry** artichokes until tender golden brown on both sides (about 6 to 10 minutes). **Drain** on paper towel. **Arrange** fried artichokes side by side in layers in greased casserole. (Artichoke slices can be prepared in advance and refrigerated until ready to use.) **Beat** together eggs, milk or cream, nutmeg, cheese, salt and pepper until blended. **Pour** over artichokes. **Bake** in preheated oven at 350° for 15 to 20 minutes or until puffy and brown. Check after 15 minutes. Serve directly from casserole. Serves 4–6.

Cook's Notes:

PARMESAN ARTICHOKES

Carciofi Parmigiani

4 artichokes	½ teaspoon salt
2 eggs, slightly beaten	⅛ teaspoon pepper
2 cups bread crumbs	1½ cups salad oil
¼ cup Parmesan cheese, grated	

Wash artichokes under cold running water. **Pull off** tough and discolored outer leaves, working from base to top. With a sharp knife, **slice** ¾ inch off top, cutting straight across. **Cut** stems even with base. With scissors, **cut** thorny tip of each leaf. **Cut** lengthwise into halves and **scoop out** fuzzy center. **Slice** each half lengthwise into 9 to 10 thin slices. **Dip** each slice into slightly beaten eggs and coat well. (It may be necessary to add more eggs.) **Roll** in bread crumbs mixed with cheese, salt and pepper. **Pour** 1 inch oil into skillet or frying pan. **Heat** over medium fire until oil is hot but not smoky. **Fry** slices in hot oil 4 to 5 minutes on each side until golden brown. **Drain** on paper towels. Serve hot or cold. Serves 4.

NOTE: Leftover bread crumbs can be placed in a jar and refrigerated for an indefinite period.

Serving suggestion: These crispy golden slices make an excellent side dish for buffets.

VARIATION: **Omit** grated cheese. **Substitute** 1 cup flour for bread crumbs.

Cook's Notes:

SICILIAN STUFFED ARTICHOKES

Carciofi Imbottiti alla Siciliana

4 medium artichokes	¼ cup parsley, minced
1 cup bread crumbs	½ teaspoon salt
¼ cup Romano or	⅛ teaspoon pepper
Parmesan cheese, grated	6 tablespoons olive oil
1 clove garlic, minced, or 1	(preferred) or salad oil
small onion, minced	

Prepare artichoke shells (see p. 185). In a bowl, **combine** crumbs, cheese, garlic or onion, parsley, salt, pepper and 4 tablespoons oil. **Mix** thoroughly. **Divide** crumb mixture into four parts. Fill center of each artichoke. **Place** upright in deep saucepan. Artichokes should fit snugly, to prevent spreading. **Pour** 1 inch water (about 2 cups) around artichokes and **sprinkle** with remaining 2 tablespoons oil. **Bring** to boil. **Reduce** fire to low and **cover** tightly and **cook** about 35 to 45 minutes or until tender. Check now and then, adding more water if needed. To **test pull** an outer leaf; if it comes off easily, they are done. **Spoon** some water from pan over artichokes. **Lift out** with two spoons or slotted spoon. Serves 4.

Serving suggestion: Serve hot or cold with green salad.

VARIATIONS: *Artichokes Stuffed with Anchovies*
Omit cheese and salt. Add 1 2-oz. can anchovy fillets, cut into tiny pieces. **Mix** with bread crumb mixture.

Artichokes Stuffed with Raisins
Add 2 tablespoons seedless raisins to bread crumb mixture. If desired add 1 tablespoon salted capers (wash before using).

Artichokes Stuffed with Pine Nuts
Add 1 tablespoon pine nuts to crumb mixture. If desired add 1 tablespoon raisins with the pine nuts.

Artichokes Stuffed with Salami
To the crumb mixture, add 2 thin slices finely minced Italian dry salami. You may substitute prosciutto, bacon or ham for salami.

Stuffed Artichokes Roman Style
Add ¼ cup chopped fresh mint or 1 teaspoon dried mint. Omit cheese and parsley.

Cook's Notes:

NEAPOLITAN ARTICHOKES

Carciofi alla Napoletana

8 small artichokes or 2 9-oz. packages frozen artichoke hearts, thawed
2 qts. cold water
Juice of 1 lemon or 2 tablespoons vinegar
¼ cup butter
2 tablespoons olive oil

2 slices prosciutto, bacon or ham
1 small onion, minced
1 lb. fresh shelled green peas or 1 10-oz. package frozen green peas
Salt and pepper to taste
½ cup chicken or beef broth or water (if necessary)

Wash artichokes under cold running water. **Pull off** tough and discolored outer leaves, working from base to top. Slice ½ inch off top, cutting straight across. **Cut** stems even with base. With scissors **cut** thorny tips off each leaf. **Cut** lengthwise into halves and **scoop out** fuzzy center. **Slice** each half into 8 to 10 thin slices. **Drop** into bowl containing water and lemon juice or vinegar. **Soak** for 15 minutes to retain color. **Drain**. **Place** butter, oil, prosciutto, bacon or ham and onion in large casserole or saucepan. **Cook** over medium fire, stirring until onion is soft but not brown (about 2 minutes). **Add** artichokes, peas, salt and pepper. **Cover** tightly. **Reduce** heat to low and **simmer** 30 to 40 minutes or until vegetables are tender. Add broth or water during steaming if pan goes dry. Can be frozen. Serves 4.

Cook's Notes:

PORK CHOPS WITH ARTICHOKES

Costatelle di Maiale con Carciofi

4 medium artichokes
1 qt. cold water
Juice of 1 lemon
2 tablespoons olive oil
4 shoulder pork chops,
about 1 inch thick

Salt and pepper
1 clove garlic, minced
½ teaspoon rosemary
2½ cups canned tomatoes
(1 lb. 4-oz. can)

Wash artichokes under cold running water. **Pull off** tough outer leaves, working from base to top. **Slice** 1 inch off top, cutting straight across. **Cut** stems even with base. With scissors, **cut off** thorny tips. **Cut** lengthwise into halves. Scoop out fuzzy center. **Cut** each half lengthwise into eighths and **drop** into bowl containing 1 qt. water and lemon juice. When artichokes are all sliced, **drain** them and **dry** with paper towel. **Heat** oil in deep skillet over low fire. **Fry** chops until brown on both sides (about 15 minutes). **Sprinkle** with salt and pepper. **Drain off** excess fat. **Arrange** artichoke slices around pork chops. **Add** garlic and rosemary, and cover with tomatoes. **Cover** and **simmer** 1 hour or until meat and artichokes are tender. If sauce is too thin when artichokes are done, cook uncovered 5 to 10 minutes until juice from tomatoes is reduced and sauce thickens. (Watch carefully.) Can be frozen. (Before freezing, cook meat only until tender but firm. Serves 4.

VARIATION: **Substitute** lamb or veal chops for pork chops.

Cook's Notes:

ARTICHOKES STUFFED WITH MEAT

Carciofi Ripieni con Carne

6 medium artichokes
1 lb. ground beef or veal or mixed pork, beef and veal
½ cup bread crumbs
2 tablespoons Parmesan cheese, grated
2 teaspoons parsley, chopped
1 tablespoon onion, finely chopped or grated
1 teaspoon salt or to taste
2 eggs
2 tablespoons olive or

salad oil
1 clove garlic or 1 small onion
1 6-oz. can tomato paste, dissolved in 2½ cups warm water
1 teaspoon salt
¼ teaspoon pepper or to taste
⅛ teaspoon nutmeg
½ lb. cooked short macaroni, or rice
Grated cheese

Prepare artichoke shells. In a bowl **combine** ground beef or veal, crumbs, Parmesan cheese, parsley, onion, salt and one egg. **Mix** well with hands. **Divide** into 6 parts and fill center of each artichoke. In small bowl **beat** other egg. **Dip** tops of artichokes in egg (this will keep stuffing compact). **Place** artichokes upright in deep saucepan or casserole. They should fit snugly to prevent spreading. **Set** aside. **Heat** oil in deep skillet or saucepan over medium fire. **Add** garlic or onion and **stir** 1 minute or until light brown. **Add** dissolved tomato paste, salt and pepper and nutmeg. **Stir** until well blended. **Pour** around artichokes. **Bring** to a boil. **Cover** and **simmer** over low fire about 45 minutes to 1 hour or until tender. Check now and then, adding more water if necessary. To **test** pull an outer leaf; if it comes out easily artichokes are done. If sauce is too thin when artichokes are done, raise flame and cook uncovered 5 to 10 minutes until sauce is thick. (Watch carefully.) **Remove** artichokes with two spoons or slotted spoon.

Place in serving dish. Serve sauce over ½ lb. cooked short macaroni or hot cooked rice. Sprinkle with grated cheese. Serves 4–6.

NOTE: Artichokes can also be baked. **Place** them in casserole or roasting pan. **Cover** and **bake** at 350° for 1 hour or until a leaf pulls out easily.

Cook's Notes:

FRIED ARTICHOKES

Carciofi Fritti

8 small artichokes   Salt and pepper
1 qt. water (approx.)   1 qt. corn oil
2 tablespoons lemon juice

Cut off about ½ inch straight across tops of artichokes. **Cut off** stems, leaving stubs about ¼ inch long. **Pull off** tough outer leaves. With palm of hand, firmly **press down** on bases to open leaves. **Scoop out** fuzzy center if necessary. **Drop** into bowl containing about 1 qt. water and 2 tablespoons lemon juice. **Let stand** 15 minutes. **Drain** upside down so all water will run out. **Shake** each artichoke and pat them dry with paper towel. **Sprinkle** centers and inside leaves with salt and pepper. **Heat** oil in heavy 3 qt. saucepan or heavy frying pan over medium fire. **Fry** artichokes in hot oil until brown on all sides, turn occasionally. **Turn** upside down and **press** tops firmly to bottom of pan, to spread leaves. **Cook** until stem can be pierced with fork (about 15 to 25 minutes depending on size and tenderness). Leaves should be as crisp as potato chips and tender enough so that whole artichoke may be eaten. **Drain** on paper towel. Can be precooked and reheated. Serve hot. Serves 4.

NOTE: Do not use shortening, butter or margerine. This Roman way of cooking artichokes dates back to the time of the Crusades.

Serving suggestion: Serve with crusty Italian bread, mixed green salad and fruit for dessert.

Cook's Notes:

FLORENTINE CHICKEN AND ARTICHOKES

Pollo e Carciofi alla Fiorentina

1 2½–3 lb. frying chicken
cut into 8 pieces
¼ cup flour
1 teaspoon salt
⅛ teaspoon pepper
2 tablespoons Parmesan
cheese, grated

6 tablespoons butter
1 14–15-oz. can artichokes,
drained
1 5–8-oz. box small fresh
mushrooms, whole
½ cup sauterne wine
½ cup chicken broth

Wash chicken under cold running water and dry with paper towel. **Combine** flour, salt, pepper and cheese in paper bag. **Shake** chicken 3 or 4 pieces at a time in flour mixture. Heat 4 tablespoons butter in skillet over medium fire. When it foams put in chicken pieces without crowding, turning as needed to brown on all sides and cook evenly (about 10 to 15 minutes). **Remove** chicken as it browns to casserole or baking dish. **Arrange** in one layer. **Arrange** artichokes between chicken pieces.

Melt 2 tablespoons butter in same skillet. **Sauté** mushrooms 3 minutes, stirring frequently. **Add** wine and broth and **boil** 1 minute, stirring to loosen any brown bits in skillet. **Pour** over chicken. **Bake** uncovered at 375° about 45 minutes or until tender. To **test,** pierce thighs or breast of chicken with tines of fork; if fork goes through easily, chicken is done. **Check** about 15 minutes before end of baking time and add about ¼ cup broth or water if necessary. Can be prepared in advance and frozen. Serves 4.

NOTE: If desired **prepare** chicken broth by cooking gizzard, heart and neck in 2 cups water, with 1 teaspoon chopped parsley and 2 tablespoons each of diced carrots, celery, celery leaves, and onion. **Season** with salt and pepper. **Cook** over medium fire for 30 minutes. Strain through fine sieve.

Rice

RICE AND CHICKEN LIVERS

Riso con Fegatini

6 tablespoons butter
½ cup minced onion
  (optional)
3 slices prosciutto
  (preferred) or ham,
  chopped (optional)
1 lb. fresh or thawed
  frozen chicken livers,
  quartered

½ lb. fresh mushrooms,
  sliced
¼ teaspoon sage
1½ teaspoons salt
⅛ teaspoon pepper
1 cup water or ½ cup
  water and ½ cup white
  wine
2 cups hot cooked rice
4 tablespoons grated cheese

Melt butter in casserole or skillet. Sauté onion for 1 minute over low heat. Add prosciutto, livers, mushrooms, sage, salt and pepper. Cook until all ingredients are well blended and livers are done (about 7 minutes), stirring frequently. Add water or water and wine. Cook 3 minutes longer, stirring constantly. Stir in rice and cheese and mix gently. Serve hot. Can be frozen. Serves 4.

VARIATION: *With Cornmeal*

With Cornmeal
Substitute 2 cups hot cooked yellow cornmeal for cooked rice. Pour hot cooked cornmeal into deep buttered serving bowl. Top with chicken liver mixture.

Cook's Notes:

RICE MILAN STYLE

Riso alla Milanese

2 tablespoons butter
1 small onion, minced
1 cup Italian or ordinary
   rice, washed
4 cups hot chicken or beef
   broth (approx.)
Salt to taste (depending
   on degree to which broth
   is seasoned)

½ teaspoon saffron steeped
   in 3 tablespoons hot
   Marsala sherry wine,
   broth or water
2 tablespoons butter
½ cup Parmesan cheese,
   grated

Melt butter in deep heavy kettle or 3 qt. casserole. **Sauté** onion over low fire 1 minute, until soft, but not brown. **Add** rice and cook 3 minutes or until every grain of rice is well coated with butter, stirring frequently. **Add** 1 cup broth and keep stirring. **Add** broth a cup at a time, stirring frequently until rice absorbs broth quickly. **Season** with salt if necessary. **Add** saffron and **stir** well. **Add** more broth and continue stirring until rice is tender (about 20 minutes). Rice should be moist and not too dry. **Add** butter and cheese and **stir** well. The complete process should take about 25 to 30 minutes. It is difficult to give exact time, since each brand of rice varies in quality. Some may absorb more broth. Serve hot. Can be frozen. Serves 4–6.

NOTE: The success of this famous dish lies in checking it every 5 minutes during cooking, and in adding the broth 1 cup at a time as the rice absorbs it. If rice is not done, add more liquid and cook longer.

VARIATIONS: *With Mushrooms*

Sauté ½ lb. fresh mushrooms (washed and sliced) or an 8-oz. can mushrooms (drained) with onions.

With Chicken Livers

Use ½ lb. fresh or thawed frozen chicken livers. Cut into eighths with kitchen shears. Sauté with 2 tablespoons additional butter for 6 to 7 minutes or until they lose their color. Add to rice during last 3 minutes of cooking.

With Truffles

Top rice with 1 truffle.

Cook's Notes:

RICE WITH LENTILS

Riso con Lenticchie

2 tablespoons olive oil or 1
   tablespoon olive oil and 1
   tablespoon butter
1 medium onion, finely
   chopped
6 cups water
1 cup dried lentils

1 small carrot, finely
   chopped
1 tablespoon parsley,
   chopped
1 stalk celery, finely
   chopped
1 teaspoon salt or to taste
⅛ teaspoon pepper
2 cups hot cooked rice

Heat oil or butter in deep saucepan. **Sauté** onion for 2 minutes, stirring frequently. **Add** water, lentils, carrot, parsley, and celery and salt and pepper. **Simmer** over low fire until soft (about 30 to 50 minutes), stirring occasionally. **Add** hot cooked rice. **Cook** 2 minutes longer. Serve hot. Preparing well in advance enhances flavor. Can be frozen. Do not overcook. Serves 4.

NOTE: This is a very nourishing dish, rich in vitamins.

Cook's Notes:

RICE WITH PEAS

Riso con Piselli

1 tablespoon oil
¼ cup butter
3 green onion tops or 1
  small onion, chopped
2 cups (about 2½ lbs.)
  fresh shelled peas or
  2 10-oz. packages frozen
  peas
1 cup raw Italian or
  ordinary rice, washed

3 cups chicken broth, beef
  broth or water (approx.)
Salt to taste (depending on
  degree to which broth
  is seasoned)
½ cup Parmesan or
  Romano cheese, grated

Heat oil and butter in deep heavy kettle or 3 qt. casserole. **Sauté** onion over low fire for 1 minute or until soft, stirring frequently. Do not brown. **Add** peas and **cook** 5 minutes, stirring constantly. **Add** rice and cook 3 minutes longer or until every grain of rice is well coated with oil and butter, stirring frequently. **Pour in** 1 cup broth or water and keep stirring. **Season** as the rice absorbs the liquid. **Continue** to add broth or water, stirring constantly. When rice is cooked (which should not take more than 20 minutes from the time the broth or water is added), it should be moist. **Stir in** grated cheese. Can be frozen. Serves 4–6.

NOTE: Makes an excellent meatless meal by omitting broth and substituting water. Season with salt.

VARIATION: 2 ozs. chopped prosciutto or ham may be added with onions and peas.

Cook's Notes:

CHEESE AND RICE CASSEROLE

Casseruola con Formaggio e Riso

1 tablespoon butter
2 slices bacon or salt pork,
cut into 1-inch pieces
1 medium onion, chopped
1 6-oz. can tomato paste
2½ cups water
¼ teaspoon salt
⅛ teaspoon pepper
4 fresh basil leaves, chopped
or ¼ teaspoon dried basil
1 eggplant (about 1½ lbs.)

¼ cup olive oil or salad oil
1 cup bouillon (any kind)
or broth
1½ cups Italian or
ordinary rice
¼ cup butter
½ lb. mozzarella cheese,
thinly sliced
¼ cup Romano or
Parmesan cheese, grated

Melt butter in saucepan over medium fire. Add bacon or salt pork and chopped onion and sauté until lightly brown, stirring frequently. Add tomato paste and water. Season with salt, pepper and basil. Cook 30 minutes. (Sauce can be made in advance and refrigerated or frozen.) Peel eggplant and slice ¼ inch thick. Heat oil in large skillet over medium fire. Brown eggplant about 2 minutes on each side. (Do not overfry.) Add more oil if necessary. Set aside.

Set aside one cup of cooked sauce. Add bouillon or broth and rice to rest. Cover and cook on low fire about 12 minutes, stirring bottom of pan gently occasionally. Add hot water if mixture becomes too dry and starts to stick. Remove pan from stove and stir in butter. Taste for seasoning. Into bottom of 3 qt. casserole, pour ⅓ of reserved sauce. Cover with half of rice mixture and top with half of browned eggplant, then half of mozzarella cheese. Repeat, ending with sauce. Sprinkle with grated cheese. To serve immediately bake at 400° oven for 15 minutes. Can be frozen. Serves 6.

RICE GENOA STYLE

Riso alla Genovese

1¼ cups uncooked rice
2 tablespoons butter
1 medium onion, chopped
1 lb. Italian sweet sausage,
with casing removed
1 cup fresh or frozen
peas
¼ lb. mushrooms, sliced, or
1 4-oz. can, drained

4 artichoke hearts, fresh,
canned or frozen, thinly
sliced
1 cup beef bouillon or broth
Salt and pepper to taste
¼ cup Parmesan cheese,
grated

Partially **cook** rice in salted water (about 7 minutes). **Drain** and **set** aside. **Brown** onion and sausage in casserole or oven-proof skillet. **Sauté** until light brown (about 5 minutes). **Add** peas, mushrooms and artichokes. **Cover** and **cook** 5 minutes longer. **Remove** from stove and **add** rice, bouillon or broth, and salt and pepper. **Sprinkle** with cheese. **Bake** at 375° 25 minutes or until rice is tender. Can be frozen. Serves 4.

Cook's Notes:

SHRIMP AND RICE ADRIATIC STYLE

Gamberi e Riso all'Adriatica

1 tablespoon olive oil
3 tablespoons butter
½ medium onion, minced
2 cups (1 lb.) uncooked
  rice
1 cup white or red wine
Broth (see recipe below)

Salt and pepper
2 tablespoons Romano
  cheese, grated

Heat oil and butter in deep heavy saucepan or casserole.
Sauté onion until soft (about 2 minutes) over medium heat.
Add rice and sauté until light golden and coated with oil and
butter mixture (about 3 to 4 minutes), stirring constantly. Add
wine and simmer 5 minutes. Add 2 cups broth, setting aside the
remainder. Cook rice 10 minutes, stirring constantly and adding
more broth as necessary. Add shrimp and balance of broth (if
balance is not 1 cup, add the difference in water). Season with
salt and pepper. Cook 5 minutes longer or until rice is tender
and shrimp is pink and firm, adding broth or water if too dry.
Rice should be moist but not soupy. Do not overcook shrimp.
Remove from heat and sprinkle with cheese. Can be frozen
until ready to use. Serves 4–6.

Broth

1 lb. uncooked small shrimp
  with shells
4 cups water
½ medium onion, sliced
1 carrot, finely diced

½ celery stalk, minced
1 teaspoon salt
1 bay leaf
1 clove garlic (optional)

Wash shrimp and remove shells. **Place** shells in large sauce-pan with remaining ingredients. **Cook** 20 minutes over medium fire. **Strain. Set aside** broth and **discard** vegetables. **Remove** veins from shrimp. Set aside.

Cook's Notes:

RICE AGRIGENTO STYLE

Riso all'Agrigento

1 cup uncooked rice	1 small onion, minced
2 cups cold water	1 can (1 lb.) chick peas,
1 teaspoon salt	undrained
2 teaspoons oil (olive oil	1 cup water
preferred)	Salt and pepper to taste

Combine rice in saucepan with water and salt. **Bring to** a boil, and **cover** tightly. **Simmer** slowly for 14 minutes. Do not remove cover and do not stir. **Cook** until tender and chewy (al dente) and all liquid is absorbed. Do not allow it to get soft. **Set** covered rice aside. **Heat** oil in separate saucepan. **Add** onion and **sauté** over low flame 2 minutes or until soft, stirring occasionally. **Add** chick peas, and juice, water, salt and pepper. **Cook** slowly 10 minutes, stirring occasionally. **Add** cooked rice and mix gently. **Cook** 3 to 5 minutes, stirring often, until rice is thoroughly heated. **Transfer** to casserole or serving plate. May be prepared in advance. Serves 4–6.

VARIATION: **Substitute** peas or lima beans for chick peas.

Cook's Notes:

RICE AND ITALIAN SAUSAGE

Riso e Salsiccia

1 tablespoon olive oil or butter
1 small onion, chopped
1 lb. sweet Italian sausage, cut into 1-inch pieces
1 lb. fresh mushrooms, washed and sliced ¼ inch thick

1 ✗2½ can tomato purée
Salt and pepper to taste
2 cups uncooked Italian or ordinary rice
¼ cup grated cheese (optional)

Heat oil or butter in casserole or deep saucepan. Sauté onion 1 minute over medium fire, stirring frequently. Turn heat to low. Add sausage and brown lightly 10 minutes, stirring frequently. Add mushrooms and sauté 3 minutes. Add tomato purée, salt and pepper and blend well. Simmer slowly about 45 minutes or until mixture has acquired consistency of thick cream. Cook rice according to recipe for Rice Agrigento (see p. 212), using 4 cups water instead of 2. Sprinkle with grated cheese if desired, and serve while hot. May be frozen. Serves 4.

NOTE: If desired, remove casing from sausage. Mix with hands and form into marble-sized balls. Brown about 5 minutes on all sides. Remove and drain on paper towel until ready to use. Drop into boiling sauce.

VARIATION: Use 1 lb. Rigatoni macaroni or Mostaccioli macaroni and cook according to instructions on package.

Cook's Notes:

RICE WITH VEGETABLES
Riso con Vegetali

1 cup dried kidney beans
4 tablespoons olive oil or
   butter
1 small onion, chopped
2 cups cabbage, shredded
1 carrot, peeled and diced
3 medium potatoes, peeled
   and diced

½ cup celery, diced
2 cups zucchini, diced
10 cups water
Salt and pepper to taste
1 cup uncooked rice
1¼ cups Parmesan cheese,
   grated

Soak beans overnight in 1 qt. water or just enough to cover beans. **Drain. Heat** oil or melt butter in Dutch oven or large heavy kettle. **Sauté** onion in oil or butter for 1 minute over low fire, stirring frequently. **Add** fresh vegetables and **sauté** 10 minutes, turning often. **Add** beans, salt and pepper to water. **Cover** and **simmer** 1¼ hours, stirring occasionally. **Add** rice and **cook** 20 minutes longer or until beans and rice are tender and most of the liquid has been absorbed. **Stir in** cheese. Serve hot. Beans can be prepared ahead of time and frozen until ready to use. Before serving add 1 cup bouillon or water if mixture is too thick. Serves 6–8.

Cook's Notes:

SICILIAN RICE

Riso alla Siciliana

2 tablespoons olive oil
1 small onion, chopped
½ lb. ground beef
1 6-oz. can tomato paste
4 tomato paste cans water
2½ cups (⅗2 can)
   tomatoes, strained or put
   through blender

1 teaspoon sugar
Salt and pepper to taste
¼ teaspoon basil
3 cups hot cooked rice
Parmesan cheese, grated

Heat oil in saucepan. **Sauté** onion over medium fire until soft (about 1 minute). **Add** meat; stir with fork until it loses red color (about 5 minutes). **Stir in** tomato paste, water, strained or puréed tomatoes, sugar, salt, pepper and basil. **Reduce** heat and **simmer** for 1 hour, stirring frequently. To serve, **place** rice in deep bowl and ladle some of sauce over rice. **Sprinkle** it with grated Parmesan cheese. **Toss** gently with two forks until rice is well coated with sauce. Pass remaining sauce. Sauce can be prepared ahead of time and frozen. Serves 4.

VARIATIONS: *With Peas*

Add 1 lb. fresh shelled peas or 1 10-oz. box frozen peas to tomato paste mixture. Excellent for buffet dinners or potluck suppers.

With Sea Shell Macaroni

Cook 1 lb. sea shell macaroni according to instructions on package. **Drain** and **place** in large serving bowl. **Add** sauce and cheese, mix thoroughly so macaroni is well coated with sauce.

RICE AND BEANS

Riso e Fagioli

2 tablespoons olive oil
1 clove garlic, minced
1 small onion, minced
1 tablespoon parsley
2½ cups (⅜2 can)
  tomatoes, strained or
  puréed in blender

Salt and pepper to taste
1 can (1 lb.) Cannellini
  beans, white or red
  kidney beans, or green
  beans
1 cup uncooked rice
½ cup Parmesan cheese,
  grated

Heat oil in saucepan. Add garlic, onion, and parsley. Sauté over low flame 2 minutes, stirring occasionally. Pour in tomatoes, salt and pepper. Simmer slowly ½ hour, stirring occasionally. Add beans and liquid and cook 10 minutes longer. Cook rice according to recipe for Rice Agrigento (see p. 212). Add to beans, mix gently and cook slowly about 3 minutes or until thoroughly heated, stirring often. Transfer to casserole or serving plate. Sprinkle with cheese and serve hot. Can be prepared in advance and refrigerated or frozen until ready for use. Reheat in casserole or in saucepan. Add more water if necessary. Serves 3–4.

VARIATION: Substitute 1 can green beans or 1 can chick peas for kidney beans. Substitute 1 cup Ditalini macaroni (½ lb.) for rice. Cook in 3 qts. boiling salted water for 10 minutes or until tender. Drain. Proceed as for rice. For added spiciness add ¹⁄₁₆ teaspoon red pepper flakes to sauce in place of black pepper.

Cook's Notes:

RICE AND BEAN SOUP

Zuppa di Fagioli e Riso

1 cup dried white beans
Water
2 tablespoons olive oil
1 large onion, minced
1 stalk celery with leaves,
  chopped
1 cup canned tomatoes or 2
  medium fresh tomatoes,
  peeled and chopped

Salt to taste
⅛ teaspoon crushed
  dried red pepper
½ cup uncooked rice
2 tablespoons Parmesan or
  Romano cheese, grated

Wash beans and **put in** deep heavy kettle. **Cover** with water and soak overnight. **Drain. Add** 8 cups water, **cover** and simmer over low fire 1½ hours or until beans are tender. **Test** for doneness by pressing a few beans with fork against side of kettle.

Heat oil in skillet. **Add** onion and celery with leaves. **Sauté** 5 minutes, stirring occasionally. Add tomatoes and cook 5 minutes longer. **Add** mixture to beans with salt and red pepper. **Sprinkle** in rice and cook about 20 minutes or until rice is tender, stirring frequently. **Stir in** grated cheese. Serve hot. Can be made ahead of time and frozen until ready to use. Serves 4–6.

NOTE: This is a thick soup with the texture of a casserole. An additional cup of hot water or broth will make a thin soup.

Cook's Notes:

SHRIMP WITH RICE

Gamberi con Riso

2 tablespoons olive oil
1 large onion, thinly sliced
3½ cups (※2½ can)
   tomatoes, undrained
1½ lbs. raw shrimp,
   shelled and de-veined

⅛ teaspoon dried basil or
   oregano
Salt and pepper to taste
4 cups hot cooked rice

Heat oil in casserole or deep saucepan. **Add** onion and **sauté** over medium heat about 2 minutes or until transparent, stirring slowly. **Add** tomatoes. **Reduce** heat and simmer 20 minutes, stirring frequently. **Add** shrimp, basil or oregano, and season with salt and pepper. **Cook** 5 minutes longer, but do not overcook. **Place** rice in individual plates or in large bowl. **Spoon** sauce over rice. Serve hot. Can be frozen or prepared ahead of time. Serves 3–4.

VARIATION: *With Peas and Celery*

Add ½ cup diced celery to onion and **sauté** 5 minutes instead of 2 minutes. **Bring** sauce slowly to a boil. Add 1 9-oz. box frozen peas 10 minutes before adding shrimp.

Lobster may also be used; **cut** into small bite-size pieces.

Cook's Notes:

RICE AND TOMATO CASSEROLE

Casseruola con Riso e Pomodoro

2 tablespoons oil
½ lb. fresh mushrooms,
   sliced
1 small onion, chopped
1 clove garlic, minced
   (optional)
¾ cup Italian or ordinary
   rice, washed and drained

1 tablespoon parsley, minced
1 8-oz. can tomato purée
3 cups water, beef bouillon
   or chicken broth (should
   be ½ inch over rice)
Salt and pepper to taste

Heat oil in large skillet or flameproof casserole. **Sauté** mushrooms over medium fire 5 minutes, stirring occasionally. **Remove** and set aside. In same oil (add 2 tablespoons more oil if necessary), **add** onion and garlic. **Sauté** until soft (about 2 minutes). **Stir** in rice and **sauté,** stirring constantly, until rice turns golden brown and is coated with oil (about 5 minutes). **Transfer** to casserole if not already using one. **Add** sautéed mushrooms and mix in parsley, tomato purée, water or broth and salt and pepper. **Cover** and **bake** at 350° for 45 minutes or until rice is tender but not mushy. Can be prepared ahead of time up to point where it is ready for baking. Can be frozen and baked for 30 minutes. Do not overcook. Serves 4.

Cook's Notes:

WHITE RICE

Risotto Bianco

8 cups water
1 teaspoon salt
1 cup uncooked rice
¼ cup butter

1 clove garlic
¼ teaspoon sage
¼ cup Parmesan cheese, grated

Place water and salt in large kettle. **Bring** to a rolling boil. **Slowly stir** in rice, **reduce** heat and **simmer** 14 to 18 minutes or until tender. During last 3 minutes of cooking, **melt** butter in small frying pan or saucepan over low fire. **Add** garlic and sage. **Sauté** until garlic is golden brown (about 2 to 3 minutes), stirring constantly. **Discard** garlic. **Drain** rice and transfer to serving dish. **Pour** hot butter over rice. **Sprinkle** with cheese. **Mix** well. Can be frozen. Serves 4.

VARIATION: Add a cup of leftover meat, poultry, or seafood.

Cook's Notes:

Sauces

BUTTER SAUCE
Sugo di Burro

½ cup butter (1 stick),   ½ cup Parmesan cheese,
   melted   freshly grated

Pour ⅓ of the melted butter over a layer of gnocchi and
sprinkle with ⅓ of the cheese; **repeat** until all gnocchi is used.
Serve immediately.

BUTTER AND CHEESE SAUCE
Salsa di Burro e Formaggio

½ cup melted butter   ½ cup Parmesan cheese,
½ cup heavy cream   grated

Stir melted butter and cream together. **Add** cheese and blend
well. Makes sufficient sauce for 1 lb. cooked and drained hot fettuccine or gnocchi.

Cook's Notes:

BASIC MEATLESS SAUCE

1/3 tablespoon olive oil
1 clove garlic (optional)
1 cup chopped onion
1 tablespoon parsley,
   minced
1/4 cup celery, finely
   chopped
8 fresh ripe tomatoes,
   chopped
2 ※3 cans Italian tomatoes
2 6-oz. cans tomato paste

1 cup water
1 teaspoon salt
1/8 teaspoon pepper or to
   taste
2 fresh basil leaves or 1/4
   teaspoon dried basil
1/4 teaspoon oregano
1 small bay leaf

Heat oil in Dutch oven or large saucepan. Sauté garlic in oil until golden brown (about 2 minutes), stirring occasionally. Discard garlic. Add onion, parsley and celery. Cook over low fire 10 minutes, stirring often. Stir in remaining ingredients. Blend well. Bring to a boil. Reduce heat and simmer uncovered until thick (about 1 hour) stirring often. Taste frequently and if sauce is too acid add 1 teaspoon sugar. Remove bay leaf from thickened sauce and discard. Strain sauce or put into blender a little at a time until smooth. Can be made in advance and frozen. To serve, simmer 15 minutes or until sauce acquires desired thickness. Makes about 7 cups.

NOTE: This sauce may be used with spaghetti, polenta, macaroni or rice. It is excellent for pizza.

VARIATIONS: *Hot Sauce*
   Add 1/2 teaspoon red pepper and omit bay leaf.

With Mushrooms
   Add 1 lb. fresh sliced mushrooms after sauce has been strained. Simmer for about 15 minutes, stirring frequently. Spoon over gnocchi, rice, or pasta, or use it for pizza topping.

With Sausage

For ½ cup sauce, **cut** ½ pound sweet or hot sausage into 2-inch pieces and **brown** on both sides over medium heat in 1 tablespoon olive oil about 5 minutes. **Add** sausage to sauce after it has been strained.

With Chicken Livers

Sauté ½ lb. chicken livers, cut into halves, on both sides in 2 tablespoons oil. **Add** livers to sauce after it has been strained. **Simmer.**

With Ground Beef

In this variation **strain** tomatoes before cooking. (Use canned tomatoes instead of fresh.) **Sauté** 1 lb. ground beef in 2 tablespoons oil, stirring frequently, until meat loses red color.

Cook's Notes:

HAM SAUCE

Salsa di Prosciutto

1 tablespoon butter
¼ lb. prosciutto or cooked
   ham, chopped
1 stalk celery, minced
1 carrot, peeled and grated
1 small onion, chopped
½ lb. ground round steak
6 chicken livers, chopped
1 bouillon cube, dissolved in
   1 cup hot water

1 cup dry white wine
2 tablespoons tomato paste
½ teaspoon salt
⅛ teaspoon pepper
⅛ teaspoon nutmeg
2 teaspoons grated lemon
   rind
2 cloves
1 cup heavy cream

Combine butter, ham, vegetables and ground round steak in saucepan. **Sauté** 10 minutes over medium fire, stirring constantly. **Add** chicken livers and **cook** 2 minutes longer. **Add** all remaining ingredients except cream. **Cook** 45 minutes. When ready to serve, **stir in** cream and **remove** from heat. Do not boil.

NOTE: Sauce may be used on spaghetti, macaroni, ravioli, noodles and gnocchi. Makes enough sauce for 1 lb. pasta.

Cook's Notes:

MAMA MIA RAGOUT SAUCE

Salsa di Ragu

1 3-lb. boneless chuck roast, rolled and tied
1 clove garlic, quartered
3 tablespoons olive oil
1 lb. fresh Italian sausage
1 clove garlic, minced
1 small onion, chopped
2 6-oz. cans tomato paste
3½ cups water
1 can (1 lb., 12-oz.) plum shaped tomatoes, mashed or puréed in blender
1 teaspoon salt
⅛ teaspoon pepper
½ teaspoon sugar (optional)
1 tablespoon fresh or ¼ teaspoon dried basil, chopped

Make 4 slits in meat, and insert quarters of garlic. **Heat** oil in large skillet over medium fire. **Brown** meat and sausage on all sides (about 10 minutes). **Remove** and **transfer** to Dutch oven or large saucepan. In same skillet, **sauté** garlic and onion in drippings for 2 minutes. **Stir in** tomato paste and water. **Blend well** and **pour over** meat and sausage. **Add** remaining ingredients, and **cook** uncovered 2 to 2½ hours or until meat is tender, turning occasionally. **Taste** and correct seasoning. When ready to serve, **slice** meat. **Arrange** sliced meat and sausage on platter. Sauce can be prepared in advance and refrigerated or frozen.

NOTE: Makes enough sauce for 1 lb. cooked and drained spaghetti or any type macaroni, gnocchi or ravioli.

Cook's Notes:

MIXED MEAT SAUCE

Salsa di Carne Misto

Meatballs

1 lb. ground beef
1 tablespoon Romano or
  Parmesan cheese, grated
1 tablespoon parsley,
  minced
¼ cup bread crumbs or 3
  slices white bread soaked
  in water and squeezed dry

1 tablespoon grated onion
1 egg
1 teaspoon salt or to taste
⅛ teaspoon pepper to taste

Combine all ingredients in bowl and **mix** thoroughly with hands. **Shape** into 12 balls about the size of an apricot. **Refrigerate** until ready to use.

Sauce

2 tablespoons oil
½ lb. (about 2 or 3 links)
  sweet Italian sausage
½ lb. beef top, round or
  chuck, in 1 piece
½ lb. pork butt, in 1 piece
½ lb. veal rump, in 1
  piece
1 medium onion, finely
  minced

1 ⅓ can Italian plum
  tomatoes (3½ cups),
  strained or puréed in
  blender
2 6-oz. cans tomato paste
4 cups water
1 teaspoon sugar
1 teaspoon salt or to taste
⅛ teaspoon pepper or to
  taste

Heat oil in large skillet. Quickly **brown** meatballs on all sides over medium fire (about 5 minutes). (Meatballs should not be cooked all the way through.) **Remove** to a large deep bowl. In same skillet, **brown** sausage, beef, pork and veal 5 minutes, turn-

ing occasionally. (If necessary add 1 tablespoon oil.) **Remove**
and **place** in bowl with meatballs until ready to use. **Strain** drippings from skillet. **Measure** 2 tablespoons drippings. (If insuf-
ficient, add oil to make difference.) **Heat** meat drippings in
large, deep heavy saucepan or Dutch oven. **Add** onion and
sauté until soft (about 2 minutes) stirring frequently. **Add**
tomatoes, tomato paste, water, sugar, salt and pepper, **stir** until
well blended. **Bring to** boil and **add** browned meatballs, sausage
and meats. **Add** any juices from meats. **Reduce** heat and **simmer** uncovered 3 hours or until sauce is thick, stirring occasionally. **Skim off** excess fat. **Taste** and correct seasonings. Can be
frozen. Serve with 1 lb. any cooked pasta. Serves 6.

NOTE: In summer, when there is an abundance of fresh tomatoes, **substitute** 2½ lbs. (about 8 medium) tomatoes for ⅓ can of
Italian plum tomatoes. **Dip** in boiling water for 1 minute. **Cool** in
running water until skin peels off. **Purée** in blender.

Another method involves **chopping and cooking** unpeeled fresh
tomatoes in saucepan over low heat 20 minutes, stirring constantly
to prevent sticking. **Cool** and strain.

Some Italians use about 1 teaspoon sugar in tomato sauce since
this helps to neutralize acid in the tomatoes. It is best to taste sauce
before adding sugar.

Cook's Notes:

TOMATO SAUCE SICILIAN STYLE

Salsa alla Siciliana

2 tablespoons olive oil
1 clove garlic
3 green onion tops, chopped
1½ lbs. ground beef or
  mixture beef, pork and
  veal
2 cups water
1 6-oz. can tomato paste

2 16-oz. cans Italian plum
  tomatoes, strained or
  whirled in blender
4 fresh basil leaves, chopped
Salt and pepper to taste
1 lb. fresh shelled or 1
  10-oz. package frozen
  peas, thawed

Brown garlic and onion tops in oil in large saucepan for 2 minutes. **Add** ground meat and **cook** 5 to 8 minutes or until meat loses red color, breaking meat up with fork. **Add** remaining ingredients except peas. **Bring to** boil. **Add** peas and **simmer** 1 hour or until thick, stirring occasionally.

NOTE: Makes enough sauce for 1 lb. short macaroni, rice or gnocchi. Pour over cooked and drained macaroni with plenty of grated cheese.

Cook's Notes:

PORK SAUCE

Salsa di Costatelle di Maiale

1 2-lb. piece pork shoulder
  or country style spareribs,
  cut into serving pieces
2 tablespoons oil
2 medium onions, sliced
½ lb. fresh mushrooms,
  sliced

1 cup dry red wine
2 cups water
1 6-oz. can tomato paste
2 16-oz. cans tomato purée
Salt and pepper to taste

Heat oil in large skillet over medium fire. **Brown** pork shoulder or spareribs on all sides (about 10 minutes). **Remove** and **transfer** to Dutch oven or large saucepan. In same skillet, **sauté** onions and mushrooms in drippings for 5 minutes, stirring occasionally. **Stir in** wine, water and tomato paste. **Pour** over meat. **Add** remaining ingredients. **Cook** uncovered over low heat 2 to 2½ hours or until meat is tender, turning meat occasionally. **Skim off** some of fat on top. Sauce can be prepared in advance and refrigerated or frozen.

NOTE: Makes enough sauce for 1 lb. cooked and drained spaghetti or any type macaroni, gnocchi or ravioli.

Cook's Note:

BOLOGNA MEAT SAUCE

Sugo di Carne alla Bolognese

½ cup salt pork or bacon, finely chopped
1 medium carrot, scraped and grated
1 medium onion, grated, minced, or finely chopped
1 stalk celery, minced
½ lb. ground beef

¼ lb. ground veal
¼ lb. ground pork
1½ cups water or stock
1 teaspoon tomato paste
Salt and pepper to taste
¼ lb. fresh mushrooms (about 10 medium), sliced

Place salt pork, carrot, onion, and celery in large kettle or saucepan. **Sauté** over medium heat for 10 minutes, stirring occasionally. **Add** meat and brown for 5 minutes, breaking up with a fork. **Add** water or stock, tomato paste, salt and pepper; blend well. **Bring** to a boil. Reduce heat; **simmer** and cook 45 minutes, stirring occasionally. **Add** sliced mushrooms and cook 15 minutes longer. Can be refrigerated or frozen.

NOTE: Makes enough sauce for 1 lb. gnocchi.

VARIATION: **Substitute** 2 tablespoons butter and 2 tablespoons oil or 4 tablespoons butter for salt pork or bacon.

Serving suggestion: Pour over cooked gnocchi and sprinkle with 2 tablespoons grated Parmesan cheese. Can be served over any type of gnocchi, macaroni, ravioli, rice or noodles.

Cook's Notes:

Wines and Liqueurs

ITALIAN WINES

The flavor of good Italian food is considerably enhanced when accompanied by good Italian wine. Italians consider wine a food, which it is; and it is very seldom indeed that an Italian meal is placed on the table without the accompaniment of some kind of wine. Sweet or dry vermouth, with a twist of lemon peel and a dash of bitters, is drunk as an aperitif. A dry red wine is usually served with a meat meal; a dry white wine with antipasto, soups, fish, poultry and pastas made without meat. Dessert wines are served with the cheeses, fruits, and pastries which end the dinner. On an especially festive occasion a sparkling wine may be drunk with dessert. After-dinner liqueurs are also consumed as part of the meal.

Wines are produced in every section of the Italian countryside, from Piedmont in the north to the islands of Sicily and Sardinia in the south. The remarkable variety and number of Italian wines reflect the widely different conditions under which they are grown, and it would not be too much to say that almost any kind of wine you might wish to drink is made someplace in Italy.

Some excellent Italian wines are imported into this country at a reasonable price, many no more expensive than our own fine domestic products. Italian wines are produced and bottled under strict government supervision, and their origin and sound quality are guaranteed by the National Institute for Foreign Trade (*Instituto Nazionale per il Commercio Estero*), whose stamp appears on every inspected bottle. You may easily and safely become acquainted with most of the types of wine that Italy exports, and a little experimentation will soon indicate which wines best meet the requirements of your own taste.

The following is a list of the Italian wines most widely distributed in America.

Red Wines

Barolo: A dry, ruby-red, full-bodied wine with a smooth, velvety taste. It is produced in Piedmont.

Barbera: A delicate dry or semi-sweet wine whose bouquet improves with age. Also produced in Piedmont.

Bardolino: A clear, light, ruddy wine, with a pleasingly dry taste. It should be drunk while still young. Made in Venetia.

Valpolicella: An excellent, deep ruby-colored wine with a delicate bouquet and mellow taste. Wonderful with any kind of meat dish. A Venetian wine.

Chianti: Probably the best known of Italian reds, this Tuscan wine has a slightly prickly taste when young which disappears as the wine ages.

Brolio: Very much like Chianti, it is grown in the same neighborhood in Tuscany. Like Chianti, also, it improves with age.

Ciro di Calabria: A deep, ruby-red wine which should be allowed to mature to develop its full flavor.

Faro: A Sicilian wine of a bright ruby color with an excellent bouquet and flavor.

White Wines

Valtellina: A light, straw-colored wine with a fresh taste. Made in Lombardy.

Terlano: A choice white wine from the Upper Audige, beautifully translucent, with an elegant bouquet.

Soave: A soft, velvety, dry wine made from grapes grown near Verona.

Orvieto: The best-known, and one of the choicest, of Italian white wines. There are two types, one dry and the other fruity. Both varieties have an attractive light-yellow color and an exquisitely delicate bouquet. From Umbria.

Frascati: A limpid, golden-yellow wine with a mellow flavor. It is also made in two types, dry and fruity. A wine of historic Latium.

Est-est-est Montefiascone: A golden wine produced near the Lake of Bolsena. Made in two types, dry and sweet. One of the most famous wines of Italy.

Lacrima Christi del Vesuvio: A straw-colored wine—sweet, velvety, and aromatic. The grapes are grown in vineyards on the southern slopes of Mount Vesuvius.

Sansevero: A fine, clear, delicate wine, excellent with fish. One of the best wines of the Apulian district.

Vernaccia del Campidano: A dry, amber-colored wine with a bouquet reminiscent of almond blossoms, and pleasingly bitter. A wine of Sardinia.

Dessert Wines

Flore della Alpi: A sweet, potent liqueur made with cinnamon sticks and rock sugar. A product of Piedmont.

Vin Santo: Golden-yellow, sweet, smooth wine of Tuscany.

Aleatico di Puglia: A red Apulian liqueur wine with a strong aroma, full taste, and pleasant, sweet flavor.

Moscato di Salento: Another Apulian dessert wine with a warm, generous, subtle bouquet.

Greco di Gerace: A delicate, smooth, golden-yellow dessert wine from Calabria, whose bouquet will remind you of orange blossoms. This choice wine is produced in limited quantities.

Marsala: The best known of Italian dessert wines. Produced in Sicily in two types, dry and sweet. It is a limpid, brilliant wine with a fine full flavor. Excellent for cooking as well as for drinking.

Nasco: A generous, brilliant, golden-yellow dessert wine from Sardinia with a delicate flavor heightened by faint undertones of bitterness.

Sparkling Wines

Asti spumante: The standard for all Italian sparkling wines. Made in Piedmont. Very delicate bouquet and a fresh, sweet taste.

Prosecco de Conegliano: A brilliant, sparkling white wine made in Venetia. It must be drunk young. It has a distinguished bouquet and a flavor underscored by a very slight trace of bitterness.

Moscato and *Lacrima Christi del Vesuvio* are also produced as sparkling wines.

LIQUEURS

Liqueurs, or cordials, are highly flavored, sweetened wines served as after-dinner drinks. They are ordinarily served at room temperature in very small liqueur glasses, for a little of them goes a long way. Italians feel that a liqueur after a heavy meal aids the digestion. Whether it does or not, the custom of sitting with friends, talking quietly, and sipping a fragrant *liquore* is without doubt a pleasantly relaxing way to end a good dinner.

Here are some of the characteristic Italian liqueurs, with suggestions for their use in cooking:

Anisette: Colorless, with an anise flavor. Use it to flavor icings and cookies. Sometimes added to highballs, pickles, frappés, and flips.

Caffe Sport: Coffee colored and coffee flavored. Use it in icings and as a sauce over ice cream and puddings.

Creme de menthe: Green or white, with a peppermint flavor. Use it in sour mixed drinks, frappés, cocktails and icings, or as a sauce for ice cream and puddings.

Grappa: Grape flavored, with a brandy base.

Maraschino: Red, cherry-flavored liqueur. Use it in icings, soufflés, and sour drinks.

Strega: Yellow, with an orange flavor. May be added to caffe espresso, or used in aromatic drinks, icings, and cake fillings.

Rosolio: Ruby colored, with a very sweet rose flavor. Made from the petals of fresh roses. Use it to flavor sour drinks, cake fillings, icings, and as a sauce over ice cream. Try a very little of it in iced tea.

All these cordials can be bought in most liquor stores, although many Italian homemakers still follow the tradition of preparing their own *liquore*. Liqueurs are a part of many Italian family celebrations. At a wedding, for instance, it is customary for the groom to offer guests a glass of liqueur, and for the guests in return to offer a toast to the bride and groom.

Index